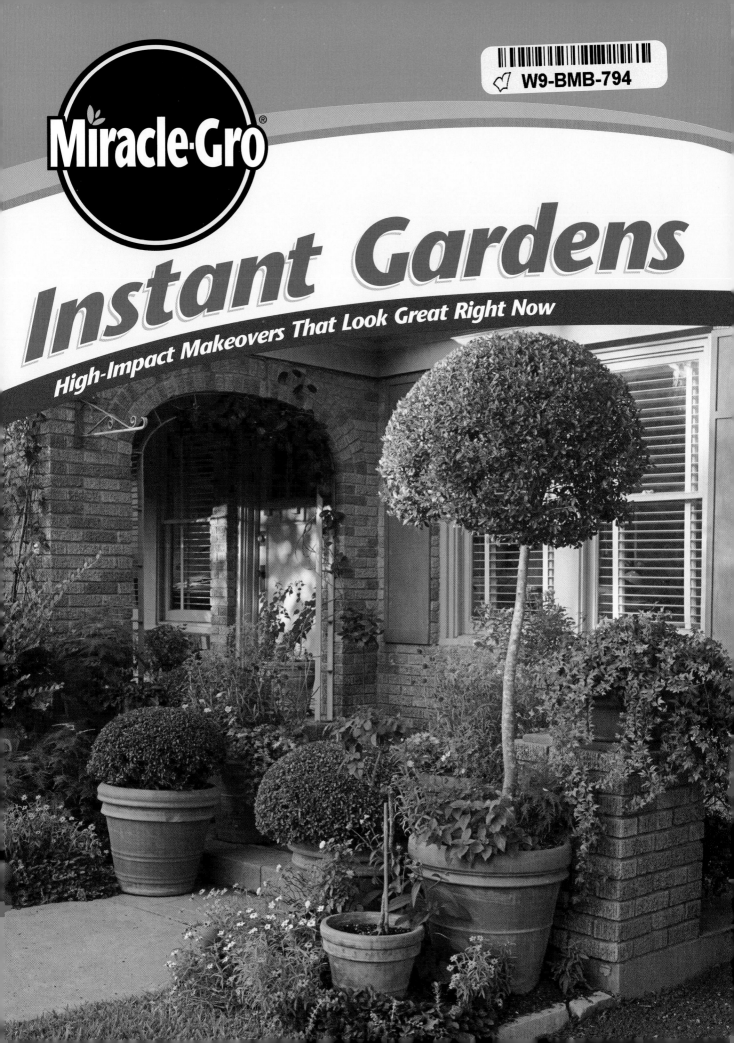

Miracle-Gro

Instant Gardens

High-Impact Makeovers That Look Great Right Now

CHAPTER ONE

SETTING THE STAGE FOR SPEED

Creating an instant garden is easy when you do a little planning. Gathering the proper tools and equipment, decking out a work space, and assembling resources at your fingertips help set the stage for speed.

In this chapter...

Using This Book

This book is designed to teach you secrets and techniques that will make an instant impact in your yard and garden.

Welcome to the world of Instant Gardens. It's an engaging notion isn't it? You snap your fingers and your lackluster yard becomes lush and colorful in an instant—like Dorothy stepping into the colorful land of Oz from her black-and-white Kansas. But can such a thing happen in gardening? Can you achieve instant results with plants that grow and bloom on their own schedule?

Yes, you can! This book is full of fast, easy, and beautiful ways to make your yard and garden look great using the secrets of professionals who achieve instant results for a living. It's packed with tips and techniques from landscape architects, garden designers, floral designers, and gardeners who transform gardens for temporary events such as garden shows as well as long-term great looks.

The first three chapters of this book introduce you to fast and easy ways to set the stage for a big event—such as a garden tour, garden party, wedding, or graduation party. Or you can transform your yard for something as important as enhancing the curb appeal of your home in order to sell it.

In chapters four and five, you'll also learn fast ways of creating longer-term effects in your garden—those that you will enjoy for years. You learn how to speed up the process of gardening—which plants grow the fastest and the tallest, the best choices for longest-lasting bloom, and which trees and shrubs look great in all seasons.

For both short-term good looks and long-term beauty, landscape and garden experts achieve fast results with plant shopping tips and planning and planting secrets such as:

- **How to drop in seasonal bloomers for quick color**
- **How to plant large trees and shrubs so they look like they've been there for years**
- **How to add or remove plantings for optimal design affect**
- **How to transform any garden using simple clean-up tricks and techniques**
- **How to pump up plant growth through feeding and pruning**
- **How to infuse color outdoors using paint, fabric, and other indoor decorating techniques**
- **How to create movable feasts of color with amazing containers**
- **How to make quick scene changes by removing poorly performing plants and replacing them with star performers**

Whether you have gardened for years or are just starting out, the ideas in this book will help you achieve beautiful results in less time than you ever dreamed. And that's what it's all about: to carve out more time to enjoy your yard, to feel pride in how your garden grows, and to be inspired with all that nature (and your local garden center) has to offer. Whether your projects involve big landscape renovations or breathing some new life into your existing garden, this book will show you fun ways to get great looks fast.

EXAMPLE IDEAS: Examples are fast, simple, and designed for gardeners and nongardeners alike. Each example shows you how to achieve a specific instant gardening possibility.

PLANT PROFILES: Fast-growing plant varieties are featured so that you can get optimum results in your gardening and landscaping work.

STEP-BY-STEP INSTRUCTIONS: Easy to follow, step-by-step instructions show you how to create fast impact in your garden.

CASE HISTORIES: These projects incorporate multiple instant gardening techniques.

DETAILS COUNT: Each example has photos of important details used in achieving an instant garden success.

AFTER PHOTOS: Completed examples show the finished results

BEFORE PHOTOS: Many of the projects have a before photo so you can see the transformation that occurs with simple, easy, and fast gardening tips.

SMART BUYING TIPS: From furniture to containers to plants, we'll show you what to look for when you are buying.

Plan Ahead

Make your outdoor
spaces as comfortable
as your indoors by
adding details such as
cushions, lighting, and
accent plants.

Dream Big!

Planning ahead allows you to deliver the
biggest punch in the shortest possible
time. It's all about keeping your eyes on
the prize.

You can garden faster and smarter if you do
some preliminary planning before you rush
out and start digging. Time is of the essence
because gardening is a time-sensitive activity.
Plants bloom on their own schedule. Because a
landscape is a living and evolving thing, you not only
have to plan for how a project will look in the ten
minutes after it is done, but also how it will look after
ten years of growth.

Planning and Planting the "Big Idea"

Every plan should start with a "big idea." "What's the big idea here?" should be your mantra as you determine what you want to achieve in your garden and yard. Your garden's big idea is essentially its theme and it can come from anywhere. House style may dictate the theme of the garden and landscaping. For example, a formal garden has specific rules with specific plantings. A very simple way to create an overall theme in a garden is to select and adhere to a color scheme. Planting all red flowers, both in beds and containers, creates a continuity that delivers the big idea of color. A big idea that communicates "whimsy" may be the simple repetition of an icon such as butterflies or fairies.

Your big idea may be one that expresses "welcome." To achieve this goal for a front yard, you can plan and plant a variety of welcoming components: Flowers flank the pathway to the house that leads visitors with unerring accuracy to the front door; colorful and fragrant blooming shrubs deliver a lovely scent; containers on the front step overflow with flowers. Even the welcome mat can be part of your scheme.

Keeping the big idea in focus during planning will help define your landscaping efforts and will deliver a consistent and unique message—your own.

Garden Planning

Interior designers carry notebooks to keep track of important decorating components: material swatches, paint chips, furniture details, completed room photos. Gardeners can adapt this idea for planning their gardens. Purchase a three-ring binder (with a waterproof cover you can take into the garden) and insert pages. Use it as part diary, part plant listing, part wish book, and part shopping list. This notebook can contain important elements for creating a plan and staying consistent to the vision you have for your yard. Here are some ways to organize your garden-planning guide to keep your big idea in focus.

A garden notebook allows you consolidate all your design, color, and plant ideas in one place.

PLANNING TOOLS

The big idea of your project should be in your mind all the time—especially when planning a change in your yard. Think about physical elements such as hardscaping, temporary elements such as containers or window boxes, and ephemeral elements such as color and scent. All these elements contribute to the big idea plan. What follows are some methods you can use to collect ideas and information before you start a garden or landscaping project.

START WITH A GARDEN MAP. It doesn't have to be professional looking—or even artistic—but a map of your garden helps you keep the big idea in the forefront.

ADD PLANT TAGS. How high will the arborvitae you planted last year grow? When you keep and collect plant tags, you have an instant garden history at your fingertips.

COLLECT IDEAS. Every time you see a photo of any element of your big idea (furniture, flowers, trees, shrubs, paving materials, arbors), cut it out and paste it in your planning book.

GATHER DREAM GARDENS. Whether they're photos from your travels or pages ripped from magazines, beautiful dream-garden images will help you keep your eyes on the prize with inspirational visuals.

Break Up Big Projects

Divide and Conquer

Breaking up big projects into smaller, doable parts is the best way to achieve big results. And achieving small successes is the best way to stay fired up about a big project.

Large landscaping and gardening projects can seem overwhelming, but if you start with small, easy-to-complete projects, you can accomplish even the biggest renovation over time. Here is a logical way to tackle a big landscaping or gardening project with multiple components.

BREAK THE TASKS INTO SMALLER PARTS

If you want to create a beautiful walkway to your side yard garden, there are two basic steps: (1) laying the walkway, and (2) planting edging plants to soften the effect. By breaking this project into two actions, you can plan, purchase materials, and do the work for each part. Whether you do them on successive days or a week apart, by breaking them into multiple actions you can accomplish more than you would ever think.

DO TASKS IN SUCCESSIVE ORDER

This sounds obvious, but ordering your project in a logical way helps you minimize the actions involved. For example, if you want to flank your front door with large, gorgeous planters, it's a good idea to position the planters where you want them and plant them on site, rather than planting and then moving them.

MAKE A LIST

Having everything at hand for a project makes it go faster. Make a list of tools, plants, hard goods, and accessory items that you need for your project. A comprehensive list helps you determine what you have at home in your garden shed, what you need to buy, and what equipment you will need to rent.

ENLIST HELP

Doing it yourself may be impossible when it comes to large-scale projects. Two hands are great. Four hands are better. There are many ways to enlist help. You can barter help with neighbors (you help them with a project; they help you) or hire high-school students or part-time laborers.

HIRE PROFESSIONAL HELP

If you have decided that you lack the skills to accomplish an aspect of a project (for example, installing electrical wires or devices), hire professional help. For landscaping assistance, contact your local garden center for quotes on garden and landscape projects. You can request quotes for drawing up garden plans and project execution as well as itemized quotes that allow you to choose the tasks you want to do yourself.

AVOID STICKER SHOCK

Like buying a new car, a landscaping project can cost a lot of money. Unlike buying a new car, however, a landscape renovation can be done in stages over time, thereby reducing the sticker shock of the project.

PIECE IT OUT

A front yard facelift can be done over time, spreading the costs of the project over a period of seasons.

1 START WITH A PLAN. Relandscaping the area around your home can be done in stages. Start with each area (front, side yards, backyard) and develop a plan that uses consistent elements. For example, if you are using brick in your front yard landscaping, using it elsewhere in the yard, such as side yard paths or a backyard patio, creates a consistent look for your entire property's landscape design.

2 BEGIN HARDSCAPING. Hardscaping elements (paths, walls, structures) are the things that most change the look of the yard. And they're often the most costly. By doing a landscaping project over time, you can enjoy some of the elements right away while saving for the subsequent phases of landscaping. For example, by adding a walkway to the front of a house in the fall, you can forestall planting costs by waiting until the following spring to plant.

3 PLAN FOR PERMANENCE. When adding a hardscaping element to your landscape, it's important to build it to last. The high price tags on good-quality stone and brick make hardscaping costly but worth it in the long run because of the long-lived nature of these materials.

4 PLANT AS BIG AS YOU CAN AFFORD. Shrubs make excellent first choices for any landscape because they are large and make the biggest impact with their ground coverage. Buying the largest shrubs that your budget can afford will give you the most immediate dramatic effect in your landscape.

5 ADD COLOR. Blooming annuals are an ideal way to colorize a new landscape. By mixing perennials into the planting plan too, you'll also be planning for the future. Although perennials may be more expensive than annuals, they come back year after year, getting bigger and better.

EXPERT TIP
If you have the know-how to do hardscaping but feel you lack the artistic talent involved in creating a garden plan, hire a professional garden designer to draw up a plan, then do the work yourself.

Phase #1

Phase #2

Phase #3

Phase #4

Phase #5

Backstage Support

In every great production, much of the magic happens behind the scenes. And gardens are no different. Behind every great garden is a great working area. That's because great gardens don't just happen. They evolve out of work done in areas behind the scenes: seed-starting areas, potting benches, growing areas, and more.

Gardening Work Areas

Storage shed, potting area, inspiration area—call it what you want, but you need a space in which to create. Be it a potting shed, a workplace carved out in an area of the yard, or a section of your garage, this is where you will keep the tools of your trade, your arsenal of special garden decorating secrets, and supplies that will allow you to transform your garden at a moment's notice. If you think of your garden as a house, this area would be the kitchen. Here are some of the basic components of a well-stocked gardening work area:

POTTING BENCH
Perfect for laying out landscape plans or starting seeds, a flat work surface is essential for the active and passionate gardener. Some gardeners even use their bench to hold laptop computers with wireless access so they can access information on planting and plant care.

TOOL STORAGE
To create a tricked-out tool storage area, visit home improvement stores and check out their garage, kitchen supply, and plumbing departments for innovative storage

Hard-working (and sometimes unattractive) planting areas can be disguised by tall-growing species such as ornamental grasses or cannas.

ideas: long-handled tool holders, magnetic-strip knife holders, and even toilet-paper holders turned sideways to dispense twine. You can instantly and ergonomically deck out and organize your garden area based on how you will use it and the type of gardening that you do.

RAMP UP
If you store wheeled vehicles in your shed or garage (wheelbarrow, lawn mower, tiller), easy access is imperative. A ramp allows free wheeling in and out of the work area.

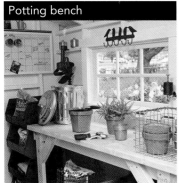

Potting bench

Toolshed

Ramp entry

Supplies storage

Reminder board/calendar	Planting screens	Shaded growing area	Heeling-in area

SHELF SPACE

Adjustable, open metal shelving allows you to match shelf height to the gear you want to stow. Keep garden food and pest-control items out of the reach of children and pets; a locked cabinet is a safe choice. If you have the room, keep one shelving unit open so you can stow last-minute yard-maintenance items such as hoses, sprayers, and other cleanup supplies before a big event. It's also a great place to keep often-referenced books, garden catalogs, and garden notebooks for instant access.

REMINDER BOARD/CALENDAR

Keep a calendar of landscaping activities and you won't have to guess when you last fertilized the lawn or started seeds. A magnetic white board allows you to display seed packets, hold canisters of screws and nails, and jot down notes about your garden that you can transfer later into your garden journal.

Behind the Scenes

Every gardener needs a place in the garden where things can be nurtured, hidden, or composted. In short, a backstage area in the garden lets you pull off a full-stage gardening production without revealing all the things that go on behind the curtain. In this space, you can position a compost pile, store soil, nurture plants on the mend, and heel-in plants while keeping the limelight on the garden. Here are backstage areas in your garden that should have a space of their own:

LIVING SCREENS

It's unnecessary for the whole world to see your work area. In the theater, the audience is kept from touring backstage. Likewise, it makes sense to pull the curtain, so to speak, across your workspace. Tall plants such as grasses or canna allow you to block unattractive but useful garden features such as bins of soil or a compost pile.

HEELING-IN AREA

A heeling-in area in your garden allows you to have a nursery space where you can temporarily plant perennial divisions, small trees, shrubs, or other plants while you are renovating a bed or border. It's also a great location to provide temporary housing for plants you get from friends or those you buy without a specific planting spot in mind.

HOLDING AREAS

The whole concept of instant gardening revolves around the idea that when plants are performing at less than their potential, they can be replaced with plants that are at their peak. While it's easy to pop plants in and out of window boxes, beds, borders, and containers, it's more economical if you can grow them to their potential in a special holding area within your garden.

AREA SHADED WITH SCREENS

A shaded nursery area is especially handy for gardeners who start their own seeds or buy plants from mail-order gardening companies. A shaded and protected area allows you to harden off plants in the spring and to shield new divisions or cuttings.

Cold frames allow you to grow a multitude of plants in cool weather. They are also excellent places to harden off greenhouse plants in the spring.

Tools of the Trade

Instant gardening techniques start with the right tools, supplies, and support facilities. Being prepared saves you time, and having what you need on hand just makes good sense.

If you were building your dream home, you wouldn't forget to add a kitchen. You wouldn't think, "Oh, I'll do the cooking in the laundry room." But that's exactly what many gardeners do when they fail to create a specialized area that makes gardening activities efficient and successful. Often, gardeners end up potting plants on their driveway, back patio, or kitchen counter—all less than desirable (and messy) places to do such a thing. Having an area equipped with the right tools and supplies is the equivalent of having a well-stocked kitchen.

THE RIGHT TOOLS

Just as with cooking, using proper, high-quality, well-maintained tools and supplies is key. Furthermore, having them where you can access them when you need them makes a world of difference in speed, efficiency, effectiveness—and even safety. For example, how many times have you searched high and low for your pruners, only to find them weeks later in a toolbox in the basement? Meanwhile, you attempt to clip flowers for a bouquet using sewing shears. In gardening as in cooking, much time is wasted trying to make do with the wrong tool, looking for a misplaced tool, or making a dash to the store to purchase a new tool because the one you own eludes you. Seamstresses have sewing rooms, woodworkers have shops, chefs have kitchens—and gardeners should have a place they (and their tools and supplies) can call home.

Storing your favorite tools in convenient locations means you'll have them when you need them—making any gardening job faster.

Trowel

Diamond-head hoe

Hand pruner

Long-handled loppers

Handsaw	Rake	Wheelbarrow	Lawn edger

Basic Tools

Check any gardening center and you'll find a host of tools. But they all do the same types of basic gardening functions. Here are the six basic types of tools.

DIGGING TOOLS

For small digging projects, such as transplanting seedlings, a **trowel** is the most useful tool. Find one that feels comfortable in your hand, is the right length to allow you to dig from a comfortable position, and is well-made. Select one that is a bright color so when you set it down in the garden, you can find it again. For large digging jobs, such as dividing perennials or planting a tree or shrub, you need a **spade**. Choose one that is the right length for your height to avoid back strain. There is a wide range of handles—D-handles, T-handles—and the best one for you is based on personal preference. For moving compost or spreading manure on a garden, a **shovel** works best because it allows you to pick up and carry a load.

CULTIVATING TOOLS

A **hoe** is the tool of choice for creating planting beds. For creating long rows for seeds, such as when planting rows of lettuce or annual flowers, a hoe allows you to dig, make planting trenches, and bury the seeds effectively. For weeding, some people prefer a **diamond-head hoe**, which allows you to slice weeds off at the root line from a standing position.

WATERING TOOLS

The most efficient way to deliver water from one place to another in your yard is through a **hose**. Look for a hose that is long enough to reach the areas in your yard where you need to water. Nonkinking types are easier to use. Keep a **hose winder** near your outdoor faucet to easily recoil your hose. Hoses become even more efficient when they are fitted with a **sprayer attachment** that directs water where you need it and allows you to change the type and force of the spray. For example, a gentle mist is preferred when watering seedlings as opposed to a blast of water, which could wash them from the soil. For wide-area watering, there are several types of **sprinklers** available. The most efficient form of watering, however, is automated **drip irrigation**.

PRUNING TOOLS

Removing dead parts from living plants is an important step in keeping them healthy and attractive. For small jobs, such as deadheading perennials or trimming out rose canes, **hand pruners** are invaluable. Many gardeners use this tool more often than any other. Invest in a pair that fits your hand (there are both right- and left-handed pruners) and spend as much as you need to—these tools will last a lifetime if properly cared for. To cut out or prune branches and twigs, such as those produced by ornamental trees and shrubs, use **long-handled loppers**. For hard-to-reach areas, use **pole loppers**. For larger branches, a **handsaw** is the safest route. And for bigger jobs, a **chain saw** is the right tool. However, it's always a good idea to contract a local tree specialist to remove large or possibly dangerous limbs or trees.

DEBRIS-COLLECTING TOOLS

Clean up garden debris in both the spring and fall when it is most excessive. A **long-handled rake** allows you to gather leaves in small areas. **Short-handled rakes** are excellent for clearing out debris under low-growing shrubs and mounded perennials. For larger leaf-gathering missions, use a **leaf blower**. And for carting compost into the garden and removing end-of-season debris, a **wheelbarrow** or **garden cart** will allow you to do the heavy lifting required of seasonal cleanups.

LAWN-CARE TOOLS

For the lawn, a **mower** is standard operating equipment. Whether it is a walk-behind (mulching models and self-propelled power options are nice) or a riding model (lawn or garden tractor), a mower produces clippings that can be bagged or mulched. A bagging attachment allows you to collect clippings, which you can use to mulch your garden. A **weed whacker** keeps the edges of your property clean—areas where your mower is unable to reach. And a **lawn edger** keeps the area where your lawn meets a hard surface, such as a sidewalk, driveway, or patio, looking neat and trim.

CHAPTER TWO

INSTANT GARDEN MAGIC

Achieving instant beauty in your garden is easy when you know the right tricks. Whether you are decking out your yard for a party or just want it to look its best right now, there are quick–fix solutions.

In this chapter...

Short Term vs. Long Term

Gardening by the rules may not always produce instant results. So break some rules. There are many creative ways to change your yard quickly.

Using instant gardening concepts in your landscaping plans can help you deck out your yard and garden quickly. And many of the things that you do for short-term effect can also grow into long-term landscaping bonuses.

SHORT-TERM RESULTS

Creating a beautiful garden in an instant seems to go against Mother Nature's plans. Plants, by their nature, have a growth plan that is difficult to accelerate. For example, you can't make a tree grow into maturity in a season. But you can fool Mother Nature with tricks of plant placement that will result in an afternoon or a week of beauty.

This is called disposable gardening. And florists and garden show designers do it all the time.

THE PRICE OF INSTANT GARDENING

Short-term garden beauty is attainable—but at a price. Of course, price is the operative word because creating an instantly beautiful and mature-looking garden often means buying plants that are bigger and more expensive, as well as buying more of them—all which increases the cost. Increased costs are the short-term compromise (but on the day of your garden party, you'll agree that it was worth it).

Also, when you plant bigger for short-term gratification, you'll also see the effects in the long term. For example, planting full-size shrubs instead of small ones offers you an instant landscape that will look good for years.

Here are a few short-term ways to break the rules to achieve instant garden impact.

PLANT OUTSIDE YOUR ZONE

Go tropical—even when you live north of the Mason-Dixon line. So what if you live in a zone where palms curl up and die with the first frost? Or where that gorgeous draping bougainvillea is five zones north of its coldest range? It's summer now, and they will both look smashing in your garden. So go for it.

GET COZY

To achieve a more filled-in look, plant closer together than is recommended. For example, if the label on the hostas you are buying indicates that you should plant them 18 inches apart, get a lusher look by reducing that space.

EXPERT TIP Some perennials take years to become fully established. To enjoy a beautiful garden while you wait, interplant slow-growing perennials with fast-to-bloom annuals of the same color.

TEAM PLAYERS

A PLANT BIG FOR FAST COLOR.
Buying fully mature, blooming plants for your gardening project is the fastest way to create instant impact. Large container plants planted in beds and borders look fully established the moment they are planted. For example, you get much more floral impact if you plant a one-gallon container petunia than if you plant a 6-pack of the same, but smaller, plants. Also, large-container, blooming perennials, such as a double hibiscus, can be dropped into a larger pot for instant decorative effect.

B USE CONTAINERS FOR INSTANT IMPACT.
You can instantly change the look of a stark patio or porch by planting a generous container packed with a pleasing combination of foliage and flowering plants. And the best thing about containers is that you can move them from place to place, wherever you need a burst of color.

C LARGE PERENNIALS HAVE LONG-TERM EFFECT.
Perennials offer long-term effect in the garden because they return year after year. Choosing tall-blooming perennials, such as ornamental grasses and Joe-Pye weed, allow you to plant large perennials that will take off to amazing heights.

D PAIR PLANTS FOR FAST APPEAL.
You can attain instant impact in the garden by planting two contrasting plants next to each other. Here both foliage shape and color create instant appeal. The arching narrow foliage of variegated ribbon grass contrasts nicely with the rounded leaves and burgundy foliage of barberry.

Quick-Change Artistry

Flower shows, such as England's Royal Horticultural Society's Chelsea Flower Show, create gardens that are meant to last a week—not a lifetime. The mirror in this archway is a clever designer's trick to create the illusion of extended space.

Garden Quick Change: an Expert View

Transform your yard and garden with tricks of the trade from experts. Smoke and mirrors? Maybe not, but close!

J. Barry Ferguson is an internationally known designer and garden events expert who creates garden and floral designs for public and private gardens. He offers this advice for making quick changes in your garden for special events.

THINK IN THE SHORT TERM

Gardeners have the parameters of climate, season, and cost. But for short-term projects, such as weddings, gallery openings, and garden shows, climate and season are immaterial. If you want a garden to look a certain way for a specific day, cost becomes the only factor. And cost can be controlled by planning.

Because an event exists for a specific amount of time, the full effect of the garden must be timed for the event. For events such as an opening, unveiling, or outdoor party, the garden must be in full and vibrant bloom, neatly clipped, generously mulched, and with not a thing out of place. "The public doesn't want to arrive to find out that the Fat Lady sings in three weeks," Ferguson says.

SEE GARDEN SHOW MAGIC

Garden shows are held in large arenas. One week, there may be a rodeo event programmed. Then the next week, the garden show, complete with fully flowering shrubs, mature trees, and trumpeting stands of daffodils must magically appear. But there is nothing magical—or spontaneous—about this type of event planning. Plants are grown for months in anticipation, and florists carefully choreograph the moment of bloom for the week of the event. According to Ferguson, garden shows bring in big plants, mulch them in, and a day later the plants are standing straight, as if to say "I look pretty; I've been here for months." This type of planning is pure science, but home gardeners can learn tricks from the experts who pull off this magical feat.

REMEMBER SHOWBIZ

After seeing a magician or illusionist, you remember only the illusion. You

A wall creates a sense of enclosure and intimacy in a garden. To get the same effect as a wall, you can use fabric or freestanding structures to create a sense of space definition.

Quick-Change Artistry
Expert Advice

For garden and flower shows, structures are built for the occasion. Here, a garden display at the Hampton Court Garden Show in England features lavender walls.

WHAT YOU CAN LEARN FROM THE EXPERTS

- Grow plants to bloom in time for the event (or buy them in full flower).

- Hide what you don't want to see in creative ways.

- Highlight what you do want to see in creative ways.

- Go for the overall effect.

- Use unorthodox materials.

- Employ the element of surprise.

- Have decorative items at your fingertips.

remember the rabbit being pulled out of the hat, the lady who escapes being sawed in half, the jet disappearing. You are less likely to remember the color of the performer's socks—or even if he was wearing any. The point is that if you offer drama, theater, and a little flashy showmanship, you can cut all sorts of corners elsewhere and nobody will notice.

AMPLIFY THE EFFECT

In the movies, computer animation can create the illusion of a large crowd of people by replicating and repeating the image of a few people. To do this on a floral level, you can employ fake flowers. "Sure, they are a cheap trick," Ferguson says, "but I use them where they can't be detected." For example, at a large outdoor garden event, Ferguson may swathe a tent pillar in cloth and stud it with roses. At eye level, all the roses you can see (and smell) are real. At the top of the pillar, the roses are silk—the same color and type as the real roses— creating the illusion that they are real.

CREATE A BACKDROP

In decorating off-site events, "You never know what you're going to have to work around until you get there," Ferguson says. So he travels with a cache of draping materials that he can use to create a backdrop or frame a view. Just like curtains on the inside of a house, draping materials can block what is in front of them (such as neighboring buildings or streets) or create a view by framing it and therefore directing the eye to it. Ferguson most often uses white, semisheer nylon organza. It is easily packed and doesn't wrinkle, and you can spread it around like frosting on a cake. Use it to festoon tent poles, make tie-back curtains, or wrap a structure that you want to disguise.

STEAL THE SCENE

Another way to create impact in the garden is to steal the scene from the rest of the garden by creating a vignette that is so striking it draws all the attention. For example, Ferguson suggests using color as a way to create an eye-catching vignette. Painting a chair or bench the same sky blue as the delphiniums and clematis that are blooming just behind it creates an irresistible look. You can create similar arrangements by grouping containers with contrasting foliage types.

LIGHT FOR EFFECT

For evening events, lights can be your best friend. Ferguson uses flood and spotlights to direct the view where he wants it. The eye can be directed to a centerpiece or focal point in the garden. And the great thing about a nighttime event is that the darkness can work in the same way a good mulch layer does—it hides the things you don't want others to see.

THINK COLOR

Even vegetable gardens can be beautiful if you consider color before you plant. Peppers add sizzle with their glossy purple, red, and yellow fruits; colored chards ('Bright Lights') offer red, orange, and yellow stems. Even beans come in wild colors such as yellow and blue. Ferguson suggests adding a "wild and beautiful scarecrow" in the middle of your garden for a finishing touch.

PROP IT UP

Ferguson keeps a wide variety of props at hand that can be used depending on the style of the party. Pedestals, rustic garden urns, gold-leafed containers, and large baskets are just a few of the items in his prop storage area. He keeps long planters that can be filled with blue lobelia for weddings—so the bride can walk up a flowering blue stairway. Another quick fix is a collection of decorative Victorian-style shelf brackets that can be tacked up anywhere to support a hanging basket instantly. And in his toolbox: nylon string for hanging artwork, aqua colored picks for fresh flowers, plastic foam, staple guns, tacky gum, raffia, ribbon, and silk flowers. He also uses rolling carts for transport.

Boxwood spheres, lavender cotton, and coral bells are planted in a rainbow arch that is an easy-to-replicate planting scheme.

Quick-Change Artistry
Your Magic Kit

Creating an instant garden is about more than just gardening technique—it's also about knowing how to shop, when to buy and when to rent, and other tips and techniques.

If instant gardening is a feat of magic, then here is a peek into the sorcerer's magic kit that allows you to pull it all off.

COVER IT UP

Some of the best tools for quick coverups can be found in your garage and linen closet. Paint resolves myriad problems with a fresh new look. Designers suggest that for painted garden elements to blend in, use white or green. To draw attention, use bright colors such as cobalt blue, orange, red, and yellow. Paint can make even the most uninspiring things look vibrant. Case in point—tomato cages: Paint them bright yellow or red to add instant impact to your vegetable garden. Fabric for outdoor use can be found in a variety of places. Old curtains from flea markets can be retrofitted outdoors to create the intimate feel of an outdoor room.

RENT PLANTS

Check the Internet and Yellow Pages for companies that rent or lease live plants for events. Many companies provide design, delivery, setup, and removal of custom-grown trees and plants. If you are looking for a grouping of topiary cypress in pots for your Italian alfresco buffet, banana or palm trees for your luau-themed party, or simply a series of lavish centerpieces to adorn tables, you can rent them all.

RENT PROPS

If you want a cage of doves cooing at your garden party (but aren't looking for more pets), try renting them. Prop rentals are an instant way to create a setting without having to own. Large-scale items such as tents, gazebos, and fountains are easy to rent. But smaller items can be rented as well, such as furniture, pots, tableware, and linens. Check out local event-rental shops first—it's their business to provide these items. If you fail to find what you want there, try antiques shops or furniture stores. If you want something special for an event but are less than thrilled about owning it forever (think doves), then inquire about rentals—even from places that may not seem obvious. You'll find antiques stores, small specialty shops, and outdoor furniture shops may be willing to rent the things you want for a fraction of the cost of buying them. Think big, then rent it.

READY YOUR RESOURCES

Keep a business-card file filled with the names of people who can help—floral designers, caterers, tree cutters, lawn services, party consultants, contractors. In a pinch, it's good to have a list of dependable people who can provide what you need. When you hear a good report about an expert, add the name to your list of resources.

Diverting and drawing attention is easy when you have the right tools. For instant gardens, you need to think as much like a magician as you do a gardener.

Heavy gauge wire

Floral wire and tape

Hooks and screws

Needle-nose pliers

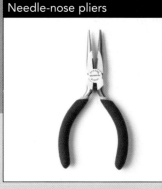

Curtain hangers

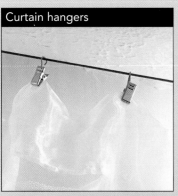

Clothespins

U-clips

Hand sprayers

Raffia ties

Hook-and-loop tape

Bamboo stakes

Plant stakes

TOOLS AND TRICKS OF THE TRADE

Your gardening magic kit may have some of the same essentials as a good home toolbox.

WIRE
Wire can be used for more heavy-duty tie-up projects, such as affixing lattice and hanging plants, candles, and art.

TAPE
Floral tape is green and thus easily hidden in the garden. For short-term fixes, floral tape holds plant material in place.

HOOKS
From tiny cup hooks used to suspend twinkle lights to heavy-duty screw-in hooks to hang more weighty objects, hooks allow you to hang it up.

NEEDLENOSE PLIERS
The perfect tool for quick fixes in the garden, needlenose pliers allow you to hold nails for hammering and can also cut wire.

CURTAIN HOOKS AND FABRIC
Transform any area into an outdoor room by hanging fabric walls. Use bamboo stakes as curtain rods. Shower curtains make excellent outdoor curtains.

CLOTHESPINS
Perfect for short-term clipping jobs, clothespins hold fabric or plant stems in place.

HAND SPRAYERS
Plants always look their best after a soft rain, so a hand sprayer is the perfect tool to apply a fresh glow of moisture to plants.

TWINE AND RAFFIA
For quick-fix tie-ups such as straightening drooping shrub branches or tying vines to stakes, twine and raffia are the best solutions.

HOOK-AND-LOOP PLANT TIES
The material that sticks to itself is perfect for propping up windfallen perennials or rain-flattened flowers.

STAKES
Easy to slip into a border, wire or bamboo stakes can be cut to the right height to make the supporting role they play invisible.

BUNGEE CORDS
For heavy-duty temporary holding jobs, use bungee cords. They're great for holding back shrub branches when it's too late to prune.

Instant Carpets

To get the most coverage when adding small plants to a landscape, buy more plants than you would normally need in the space and plant them closer together.

Flowers and Color

Once you've gotten your planting tools and plans in place, it's time to dig in. For fast-fix landscaping, use ground covering, bedding plants, sod, mulch, and stone.

Your local garden center has magic carpets for your yard and garden. Depending on what you want to do—plant a garden bed, create a walkway, connect one place in your yard to another—there is a host of quick-coverage materials that can provide dramatic and instant results.

COLOR CARPETS

At certain momentous times you may need instant and inspirational color in your garden—alfresco dinner parties, garden tours, weddings, graduations. If you need instant flower color for a special event, then annuals will become your best gardening friends. Bred to bloom with gusto, these flowering powerhouses can be purchased in bulk at any garden center. Flats of annuals are usually discounted, so in addition to getting a lot of color, you're also getting a good deal.

BIG AND BLOOMING

When you buy flats of annuals, purchase only the ones that are in full bloom. If you are planting well ahead of the event, you may opt for plants in bud. But if you are planting for instant impact, you need plants already doing their stuff. Choose the largest plants you can get. Flats hold plants grown in four-packs and six-packs. Plants in four-packs are larger and will be more impressive in the ground or packed into containers. If you have a choice, buy bigger plants.

SEEING DOUBLE

The first rule of planting annuals for instant impact color is to plant them closer together than their plant tag spacing recommendations indicate. By packing them into the garden, in a slightly more spaced-out version of a flat, you create an illusion of a carpet of color.

BORN TO SPREAD

There are a number of annuals that excel in fast coverage: Wave™ Series petunias are engineered to spread and flower with wild abandon. They do better in hotter weather, as do moss rose, melampodium, and cupflower.

BRIGHTER IS BETTER

Another optical illusion that you can perform in your garden is to buy bright-colored plants. Their strong colors give the effect that there are more of them than meets the eye, which is a good thing when it comes to flowers.

COLORFUL COVERAGE

A PETUNIAS

An old favorite with new varieties, petunias are one of the fastest ways to a colorful cover-up. 'Wave' Series petunias are rapid growers and swift spreaders. Available in a wide range of colors and bicolors, 'Wave' petunias are versatile hanging basket plants and window box choices. By using a large hanging plant as an inground planting, you can easily cover a foot or more of ground in blooms. These petunias love hot weather and will bloom generously without deadheading.

B LOW AND BEAUTIFUL

Low-growing mounds of lavender moss phlox are the perfect carpet for a gate entryway. In the early spring, this thick-matting, sun-loving groundcover is wall-to-wall flowers. You can buy flats of moss phlox at garden centers in thick, sodlike chunks that are easy to plant and look great immediately.

C FLOWERS AND FOLIAGE

Low-growing and shade-loving flower and foliage pairings make excellent edging choices for shady borders. Hostas are versatile groundcovers that come in a wide range of colors (green, variegated, chartreuse, blue, and yellow), leaf types (puckered to smooth), and sizes (tiny edging plants to back-of-the-border monsters). Their classic leafy good looks are enhanced when planted with showy annuals such as vinca and begonias.

D BLOCKS OF COLOR

Bedding annuals, such as red salvia, are nature's version of wall-to-wall carpeting. Closely-planted annuals add instant color when they are planted in large blocks or swaths of color. When buying annuals for an instant impact garden, choose ones that are stocky and in full bloom.

Instant Carpets
Sod and Mulch

Rolling out sod onto a barren area or distributing mulch around plants creates instant impact coverage and provides continuity.

Patching new grass into an existing lawn is easy. Just remove the sod, spread a base of soil (such as Scotts® Premium LawnSoil), and heavily seed the area with grass seed. Grass sprouts quickly. Make sure to keep it well watered so that it can establish a good root system.

Roll-Out Lawn

You need fast coverage when you are looking for instant impact results. For lawns, seeding is cheaper, but sod is instant. When it comes to instant cover-ups in beds and borders, mulch is the way to go.

There are two reasons to add sod to a yard: to lay a bright green carpet down where nothing existed before, or to redo an area of grass that has become sparse, overly weedy, or both. Either way, sod is a great way to make a fresh green start.

Sodding is only slightly more difficult than spreading a throw rug on a hardwood floor. Clean the area, roll the sod out like a carpet, then water it in. Unlike a new rug, you should keep from walking on sod immediately after it is laid, so avoid laying it in an area where it will receive a lot of foot traffic before it is well-established—usually a couple of weeks.

Rolling out sod is easy and the fastest way to have a great looking lawn in the least amount of time.

Line up the sod rolls before you unroll in order to keep straight lines.

Fast Coverage: Mulch

Mulch is about as instant as it gets. It is the gardening equivalent of hiding dirty dishes in the oven before guests arrive. Mulch refers to any material you spread on the ground to cover the surface of the soil. In addition to covering up, mulch helps unify areas. But mulch has even more benefits. It helps suppress weeds, conserves soil moisture, reduces erosion, and protects plants in the winter.

Mulch under trees out to the drip line. A clean edge around the mulch makes mowing under trees easier, too.

ORGANIC MULCH—PLANT MATERIAL BYPRODUCTS

1 PINE STRAW The dried needles from pine trees creates a lovely forest-floor feel. They're also the perfect, natural mulch for acid-loving plants such as azaleas and camellias.

2 COCOA HULLS Lovely rich-brown cocoa hulls (often smelling slightly of chocolate) are a small, lightweight mulch that is perfect for spreading around small or low-growing plants such as newly planted herbs. Cocoa hulls decompose readily, which means you must reapply them often.

3 BARK NUGGETS Bark nuggets are made from pine and fir trees and are attractive and fairly resistant to decomposition. They are often available colored in shades of red, brown, or black.

4 GRASS CLIPPINGS If you have a lawn, you have a never-ending supply of grass clippings. As you mow, collect lawn clippings in a bag. Allow them to dry to a straw-colored mulch, then apply them to the ground around your plantings. They're perfect for vegetable gardens. Avoid using clippings from grass that has been treated with a broadleaf weed killer.

5 SHREDDED WOOD Both hardwood and softwood trees can be shredded for bark mulch. Avoid mulch made frrom recycled wood that may be contaminated with CCA (copper chromate arsenate) by looking for the Mulch and Soil Council certification on the packaging stating that the product is made from natural forest products and contains no recycled wood or contaminants.

INORGANIC MULCHES—FOR LONG-LASTING COVERAGE

1 SLATE Dark and uniform in color, slate offers a more exotic look than river rock. It is, however, more expensive than other types of rock. It is often used in Asian-influenced gardens because of its color and texture.

2 RIVER ROCK Rounded river rocks come in a variety of sizes. When spread over landscape fabric, they serve as a permanent, low-maintenance mulch.

EXPERT TIP If your bark mulch is in good shape, but just a little faded, you can refresh the look by using mulch dye. Sprayed over existing mulch, the dye, which is harmless to your plantings, gives it a fresh-from-the-tree look.

Instant Carpets
Brick and Stone

A threshold made of rotting wood is not only unattractive—it's also potentially hazardous. Replacing a worn wood step with stone offers a long-term solution that also looks great.

BEFORE

TIME NEEDED
4 to 6 HOURS

AFTER!

Walk This Way

Few surfaces add as much permanence and warmth as brick, brick pavers, and flagstone walkways and patios. Surprisingly, you don't need to hire a professional to lay these instant walkways.

Walkways are more than just a convenient way to get from the street to the front door or a way to traverse a yard or garden. A path adds instant appeal as well as a sense of destination to any yard. Paths are also structural elements that add grace and form to any landscape. Whether a formal straight path or a more casual curved route, a walkway of flagstone, brick, or paving stones is easy to lay down and virtually indestructible and immovable, and it lasts for years.

Paths that are made from long-lasting materials such as stone are more formal in nature. You can also construct paths of less solid materials, such as wood chips, pine needles, or pea gravel. However, these materials are difficult to shovel in snowy areas and are easily spread throughout the lawn or into the garden by people and pets. So for the most permanent path options, go with stone or stone look-alikes.

1

2

3

4

5

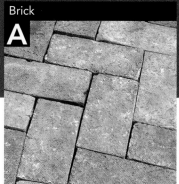
Brick

A

Crushed brick and concrete

B

Flagstone

C

Treadable groundcover

D

THE SIMPLE STEPS: RIVER-ROCK THRESHOLD

1 LEVEL THE AREA. After you have removed the existing threshold material, level the stepping area using a hoe. Add a 2-inch layer of sand.

2 ADD THE FLOORING MIX. Using a dry mixture of sand and concrete, create a flooring layer on which to place the river stones. Smooth the dry mixture with your hand or a rake.

3 LAYER THE BASE STONES. Place a layer of flat stones side by side to form the bottom layer of the step. To hold the stepping stones in place, position edging stones to form the entire base of the step. Pour a layer of the dry concrete mixture over the top of the stepping stones.

4 SPRAY IT DOWN. Using a hose, spray water onto the concrete mixture to help form a solid base for the step. Make sure all the dry concrete mixture is moistened.

5 APPLY TOP STONE LAYER. Add a layer of stones, side by side, on top of the moistened concrete mixture and allow it to dry.

THE FLAGSTONE PATH

6 CREATE A PATTERN. Place the stones or pavers in the pattern you've selected. Simple patterns require less sod cutting.

7 DIG IT OUT. Dig the walkway or patio area to a depth of about 5 inches plus the depth of the paving material. If digging a patio, make sure it slopes slightly away from the house.

8 SPREAD A BASE AND LEVEL THE SAND. A 4-inch base of gravel or crushed concrete creates a level bed for the stones to sit upon. Distribute the gravel evenly with a rake; then tamp it firmly into place. Lay down a sheet of landscape fabric to act as a weed blocker and a foundation for a 1-inch layer of sand that you put on top.

9 INSERT THE STONE. Place the stone into the space. Tamp it down into place firmly by standing on it.

PAVER CHOICES

A BRICK
A classic, sometimes formal look, brick offers beautiful earth-toned rectangles that can be laid in a number of patterns. Brick is the ideal medium for laying a straight or arching path.

B CRUSHED BRICK WITH CONCRETE
Combining two paving choices creates visual interest. Here, round concrete steppers are combined with crushed brick. The concrete offers a stable walking surface and the crushed brick surrounding the concrete allows for a wider path as well as a way to block out weeds around the pavers.

C FLAGSTONE
Either set in sand the way bricks and brick pavers are, or cut into the lawn as stepping stones, flagstone offers large, flat, irregular, and interestingly shaped stones that make ideal footpath materials. Flagstone can be cut and sized to fit any area. Its light color makes it an ideal partner for red brick or stone pavers.

D TREADABLE GROUNDCOVERS
Adding small, treadable groundcovers that grow between the cracks of stones or brick is an instant way to make the area look established. Creeping thyme, small sedums, lilyturf, and mondo grass are good underfoot options.

6

7

8

9

Cleanup Basics

BEFORE

AFTER!

Simple nipping and
tucking makes neat
work out of this
landscape.
Deadheading spent
blooms, trimming
yews and barberries,
and sizing back
burning bushes makes
a big impact in a small
amount of time.

TIME NEEDED
4 to 6
HOURS

Sometimes
a quick
cleanup is
the fastest
way to a
better-looking
landscape. A few
hours of pruning and
deadheading can
totally spruce up
a landscape.

Even well-cared-for plants need to be maintained with pruning, trimming, and deadheading. Unless you live in the tropics, you need to trim only once a year. That's the good news. The other good news is that overall, yard cleanup tasks are easier than you think. Here are the essential cleanup techniques.

DEADHEADING

Removing the spent blooms from plants cleans up their look and improves their performance. Annuals such as marigold, geranium, snapdragon, and fuchsia all look better, and bloom longer, when you deadhead. Perennials also can be deadheaded to improve flowering. Hostas, for example, send up spires of blooms, which may or may not be desirable. They can be pruned off at the plant crown. And flowering shrubs such as rhododendron, azalea, and lilac all look better with the faded blooms removed. Snap off dead blooms where they join the stem—just below the flower head.

PRUNING DECIDUOUS SHRUBS

Leafy shrubs such as burning bush, barberry, and viburnum all benefit from occasional pruning. Remove any dead wood using sharp pruners or loppers. Also remove broken or diseased branches. Then cut back overgrown branches. You can remove about one-third of the overgrown stems. Cut them back to the base and remove any branches that may cross or rub against one another.

TRIMMING EVERGREEN SHRUBS

Evergreen shrubs come in two basic types: narrowleaf or needled evergreens, which include pines, yews, and junipers; and broadleaf evergreens, which include holly, boxwood, and rhododendron. Remove any dead, broken, or diseased branches on a regular basis. General pruning is best done in late winter or early spring before new growth begins. It's best to prune annually so you can avoid having to do severe cutting, which can mar the overall look of the shrub. Yews can be trimmed into rounded or square shapes by using a hedge trimmer.

REMOVING PLANTS

Remove any dead or diseased plants in the landscape. Use a chain saw to remove large branches and trunks. When all of the foliage has been removed, dig out the root ball before planting healthy replacements.

MOWING

Obviously grass needs to be cut. But mowing also has health benefits for a lawn—and immediately noticeable instant impact results. A freshly mown yard looks greener, and mowing helps the grass stay thicker, which in turn helps choke out weeds that negatively affect the overall lushness and consistency of a lawn's look. Regardless of the type of mower you use (riding, push, electric, gas-powered), the cutting blade on the mower should be set high—about 3 to 4 inches—for healthy grass. It's especially important in the hot months of summer to cut high. A scalped lawn is less resistant to weeds and drought conditions.

HAND PRUNERS are used to prune small branches, flower stalks, and weeds up to 1 inch diameter.

LOPPERS are for branches that measure up to 1½ inches. Lopping shears allow you greater leverage.

CHAIN SAWS, (gas- or electric-powered) should be used for branches larger than 4 inches.

LONG-HANDLED SHEARS allow you to trim out parts of dense hedges such as privet.

ELECTRIC HEDGE CLIPPERS are the perfect tool for taking a little off the top.

It's a common problem. Junipers grow larger every year until they outgrow the space they were planted in. To cut a large juniper or yew down to size, do more than cut off the top and sides. Prune from the inside, removing large branches at the base, while still keeping the shrub's shape. Long-handled loppers are the best tool for this job. Proper pruning reduced this juniper by nearly half.

BEFORE

AFTER!

Cleanup Basics
Border Patrol

BEFORE

No More Boring Border

TIME NEEDED
2 to 4
HOURS

Creating a beautiful flowering border is faster than you think. Start with a clean edge and pack in blooming plants for a fast renovation to a border that has lost its appeal.

AFTER!
A border is transformed into a color-coordinated planting bed that dresses up a side yard for three-season appeal.

1

2

3

LAYING A STONE BORDER

1 PREPARE THE SURFACE. Remove existing edging and rake the area smooth. At the border's edge, create a shallow channel for the stones to sit in.

2 DETERMINE STONES NEEDED. Measure a straight line of about 6 feet. Line up the stones and multiply by the border's length to determine the total number needed for the entire project.

3 POSITION RIVER STONES. Add the stones to the trenched area. Amend the soil with compost or peat moss for planting.

WHAT TO GET

MATERIALS

- River or field stones
- Soil amendments
- Spring-blooming bulbs
- Summer annuals
- Perennials

Time marches on—and in a landscape, that's both the good news and the bad news. For plants, time is a good thing. It causes small, inexpensive shrubs to grow tenfold (and maybe more) into lush mature plantings. Time also softens the look of new brick and freshly laid stone with a patina of age, making it look more attractive and established. But time also causes wear and tear. The longest-lasting landscape elements, such as edging, steps, and stone, can shift or rot over time. Weather extremes and temperature shifts cause natural breakdown of even the most solid materials—and create the need for a fresh look.

BORDER PATROL

Cleaning up an existing border starts with a frank assessment of the border's components. If the edging is rotting, the bed weedy, and the plants in need of division, the easiest way to renovate the bed is to start over. But that sounds worse than it is. Using basic quick cleanup techniques, you can create a stylish border in a weekend. And here's a secret. Once the bed is planted, mulched, and looking great, the upkeep is easier than spending the summer weeding and maintaining a less-than-luscious garden. Choosing between an unadorned wall and a gorgeous bed is easy.

TIME-RELEASE PLANTINGS

Enjoy low-maintenance seasonal color by creating a time-release planting plan. By planting early risers such as grape ivy, squill, and daffodil, you fill the border with color starting in early spring. As the small bulbs finish blooming, spring perennials such as large-leaved peonies send up foliage sprouts, which cover up the dying bulb foliage (no cleanup involved). After the peonies have bloomed, add blooming annuals such as coleus and wishbone flower to brighten the border until frost. With nearly every square inch of ground planted, it's hard for weeds to get a roothold. Mulching the bed also helps keep it weed free.

PLANTING FOR MULTISEASON COLOR

By layering plants and bulbs, you can enjoy multiseason color—from early spring through frost.

SPRING

BLUE AND PINK THEME
GRAPE HYACINTH (MUSCARI SPP.)
HYACINTH (HYACINTHUS ORIENTALIS)
SQUILL (SCILLA SPP.)
STRIPED SQUILL (PUSCHKINIA SCILLOIDES)
DAFFODIL (NARCISSUS SPP.)
PEONY (PAEONIA SPP.)
HELLEBORES (HELLEBORUS SPP.)

SUMMER/FALL

PURPLE AND RED THEME
COLEUS (SOLENOSTEMON SCUTELLARIOIDES)
RED CELOSIA (CELOSIA HYBRIDS)
PURPLE OR PINK WISHBONE FLOWER (TORENIA FOURNIERI)

Cleanup Basics
Side Yard Spruce-Up

BEFORE

Creating an Edge

TIME NEEDED
2 to 4 HOURS

An overgrown, shaggy-looking side yard garden gets a fast afternoon makeover. Edging adds definition (and a barrier) from messy invading turf.

AFTER!
Adding edging and mulch cleans up an existing bed, defining it from the lawn (and the inevitable grass creeping in).

WHAT TO GET

MATERIALS

- Spade
- Pruners
- Hammer
- Plastic edging
- Landscape fabric
- Mulch

GETTING AN EDGE ON THE GRASSY COMPETITION

1 ESTABLISH THE BED'S EDGE. Using a sharp spade, slice into the turf to define the edge of the garden bed.

2 PEEL BACK SOD. To effectively remove the grass from the garden's edge, peel back the sod, removing roots and all.

3 MAKE A CLEAN EDGE. Cut a clean edge for the edging to rest against, making a small trench to stabilize it. Make sure it is deep enough so the edging is flush with the ground. Cut the appropriate length of edging for the garden bed. Plastic edging is flexible and can go around corners, and it can be cut easily with pruning shears. Place the edging in the trench, snugging it up against the side of the lawn.

4 TACK IT DOWN. Hammer in edging spikes to hold the edging in place. Replace the soil, leaving 2 to 3 inches for mulch.

5 LAY LANDSCAPE FABRIC. Spread landscape fabric over the bed, cutting holes to accommodate existing plants.

6 TOP WITH MULCH. Layer 2 to 3 inches of fresh mulch on top of the landscape fabric to prevent weeds or grass from sprouting in the garden.

It happens to the best gardeners. A garden bed gets overrun with grass, and pretty soon it's hard to tell where the lawn ends and the garden starts. Grass, by its very nature, likes to spread. But when it invades the garden beds, it's time to take action.

ON THE EDGE

For a crisp, neat definition between bed and lawn, black plastic edging offers many benefits. It's easy to install without special skills or equipment. The only tools you'll need are a spade, a hammer, and hand pruners. When you are done installing the edging, all you should see are the clean lines it creates. The ultimate goal of a good edging job is to see only the edge, rather than the edging.

Edging is especially useful when you mulch beds and borders, because it creates a barrier that keeps the mulch from spreading into the lawn. It should be installed at ground level so you can mow over it without nicking the top with the mower blades. Look for heavy-duty polyethylene edging that has a rounded top and a series of grooves on the bottom to help prevent it from being heaved up by frost. Polyethylene is a flexible material that allows you to make graceful curves where needed. It is sturdy and won't stiffen and crack in temperature extremes.

OTHER EDGING OPTIONS

A wide variety of edging options is available. Steel and aluminum edges work like plastic edging. Inserted into the ground, they create a ground-level edge that stops grass and weed invasions. Stone or brick can be used as edging—inserted into the ground or set on the ground depending on the style of the garden you have. For example, bricks or limestone squares inset into the ground are appropriate for more formal gardens. Mowing maintenance is easiest with this type of edging because the mower can roll across the edging without it catching the blade. You can also set bricks on their sides at an angle for a more decorative look. For country or less formal gardens, stones set on the ground make an attractive edging. To make this kind of border more naturalistic, use varying shapes and sizes of stone. For lawn maintenance, use a weed trimmer to keep a clean edge. Upright pieces of wood or horizontal timbers make a rustic edge.

Portable Plants

A B
C D

Container plantings allow you to serve up flowers and foliage anywhere you want—on patios, terraces, porches—even in garden beds and borders. Containers offer you the ultimate in instant impact color.

Container gardening is the great gardening equalizer. Regardless of how small your garden space or your climate or soil type, you can create the perfect environment to grow anything you want—all in the confines of a container. You select the potting-soil mixture, you control the amount of water it receives, and you place it in the type of light that it needs. Grow bananas in Iowa? No problem! Cultivate cactus in Seattle? Go ahead! Besides being portable to any location, container gardens allow gardeners to grow plants that usually fail to thrive outside their respective climates.

Container gardening also allows gardeners to orchestrate artistic matches between pots and plantings. In fact, the pairing of containers and plants allows you to make horticultural and design statements that plants alone in the garden are unable to make. Containers literally and figuratively elevate the flowers or foliage planted in them. Terra-cotta pots offer a neutral palette. Ceramics come in colorful options (available in solid colors or enhanced with objects or multicolored washes). Natural stone containers add a sense of timelessness. Even found-object containers such as wooden boxes, vintage wire baskets, or galvanized buckets can be employed as vessels for your favorite flowers and foliage.

SINGLE CONTAINERS

Container gardening allows you to highlight individual plant species or combine your favorites into small self-contained gardens. Even small containers can impart great impact. For example, a black ceramic bowl filled with multihued succulents and topped with white water-smoothed stones creates a minimalist (but stylishly mighty) centerpiece. A barrel-size painted glazed ceramic planter with a wild assortment of grasses serves as a garden focal point—and end-of-path destination. Single containers can also carry a home's style into the garden. For example, if a home's exterior is Mission style, angular, stylized planters can echo that style in the garden.

POT COMBOS

Clustering containers into groupings is a great way to amplify the effects of the flowers and foliage. Using the same tenets of design as you do in the garden, you can combine containers of different heights, sizes, and colors and fill them with varying leaf and flower forms, textures, and sizes to create a diverse visual masterpiece. Color themes, such as a blue-and-white delftware theme, are popular for container groupings because both the plants and the pots add their power to the scene. Clustering containers on a patio or porch, or using them to dress up a bare wall, also allows you to water them all at once, saving time and water. Their physical proximity protects them from drying winds.

COOL CONTAINERS

A COMBINE TEXTURES
Get textural in your next container planting by choosing plants from the large family of succulents: Blue-hued echeveria and tightly coiled hen and chicks are interspersed with smooth white and black stones for a relaxing Zen effect in a pot.

B AMPLIFY THE EFFECT
Grouping containers is a great way to amplify their effect—especially useful if you have lots of small containers.

C LOOK HERE!
Containers can hold their own as a simple but effective garden focal point. This pleasing pairing of a yellow-and-blue striped pot and spiky dracaena foliage makes a stunning statement without a bloom in sight.

D MIX IT UP
Annuals provide a paint box of colorful options for container gardeners. Here, purple petunias bloom next to fragrant white dianthus and gray-blue licorice plant.

HIGH-FLYING FLOWERS
Flowers and foliage suspended overhead are an instant impact way to add color to empty air. Hanging baskets packed with flowering annuals and vines create decadent draperies of bloom. Lush, flower-filled hanging baskets can dress up a porch in foliar finery and soften the angular edges of a patio or terrace.

CONTAINERS AND MORE
Containers can offer more to gardeners than just a way to add color. They can also add structure and height to an area by providing a perch from which a vining plant can climb. For example, even a simple terra-cotta container can be elevated to new gardening heights by inserting a rustic branch tuteur or formal tepee into the base and allowing a fast-growing vine to twine.

Portable Plants
Houseplant Hideaway

Your houseplants love having a summer vacation outdoors, but how do you find the space for them all? Create a tropical paradise on a deck or patio in an instant by grouping plants together in amazing ways.

BEFORE

Gardeners who have rooms full of houseplants have to look no further for outdoor decorating inspiration. Most houseplants originated in tropical climates and offer a sumptuous palette of leaf textures, colors, and shapes to use in creating a lush patio setting. Simply moving indoor plants outdoors improves their health and appearance. (Most houseplants will do best in a partially shaded area.) But grouping

AFTER!
Create a tropical patio getaway by moving your houseplants outdoors and grouping them in creative ways. Annual flowers and throw pillows add touches of color amid the jungle of greenery.

them in creative ways allows them to shine.

The key to making your porch or patio a tropical paradise is to group the houseplants together so that they make both a vertical and horizontal statement. For example, plant towers, structures that hold a variety of potted plants, are the perfect way to display many hanging plants—and the simple grouping of multitextured plants makes a stunning centerpiece. Even the tiniest houseplants can be bit players in the tropical drama when they are grouped together in deck-rail planters.

Adding a mulch of oranges or other colorful citrus fruits dresses up a large pot.

A

B

C

D

E

LUSH LEAVES IN TEXTURES, SHAPES, AND COLORS

A BIG AND BOLD leaves, such as those spotted dumb cane produces, offer an instant tropical infusion for patios. Other large-leaved houseplants include philodendron, peace lily, fatsia, and schefflera.

B LIGHT AND AIRY leaf textures offer a soft and lacy look. Tiny-leaved asparagus fern is happy both indoors and out. Other houseplants with airy foliage include aralia, Norfolk Island pine, podocarpus, and other ferns.

C THICK AND SUCCULENT leaves, such as those produced by jade plant, add an exotic element. Other plants that feature succulent foliage are donkey's tail sedum and portulacaria.

D SLENDER AND SPIKY leaves give the appearance of a fountain. These leafy sprays can be found with dracaena, snake plant, and New Zealand flax.

E COLORFUL SWIRLS, such as the variegation found in the round leaves of peperomia, are best used in combination with plainer plants to heighten their swirly appeal. Other multi-toned foliage houseplants include croton, begonia, variegated English ivy, and caladium.

Portable Plants
Small but Powerful

Small houseplants take on a big presence when they are grouped together in planters. Mix different leaf textures and colors to create foliar fantasies.

Small Plants Make a Big Impact

TIME NEEDED 1/2 to 1 HOUR

The old axiom "strength in numbers" is especially true when it is applied to small plants. Indoors, in the small space of a room or windowsill, houseplants can be admired for their intricate details. But in a large outdoor space such as a porch or patio, their tiny stature makes them seem insignificant. Group them together, however, and even the smallest of plants can make a big statement. Combine different types of houseplants to create a foliage sum that is truly better than its parts.

1 ADD A LINER FOR LOOKS. Matted fiber liners are perfect cover-ups for pots. Insert them into any wire or wrought-iron planter for an instant nest to hold your vacationing plants. You can buy fiber pot liners that are form-fitted to individual planters, or you can purchase fiber material in sheets and cut it to fit the container.

2 HUDDLE YOUR HOUSEPLANTS. Combine interesting leaf textures and colors by inserting individual small potted houseplants into the lined planter. Arrange the pot positions until you like the look. It's important to water plants in pots more often than you would water plants in the ground. Feed houseplants on a regular basis. Before frost, lift the houseplants out of the planter and return them to their indoor homes until the following spring.

Tower of Power

Arrowhead vine

A

Hanging houseplants have somewhere to stretch their legs when you bring them outdoors and mass them together into a tower of foliage. Group plants with similar light and watering requirements together for easier care. You can turn potted plants into hanging plants by attaching a wire hanger around the rim of the pot. Pot towers come in a variety of styles and materials and look great both indoors and out. Heavy-duty iron towers weighted down with pots can stand up to most outdoor winds without tipping.

Dracaena

B

Peperomia

C

OTHER PLANT PICKS

Mix it up! Mass single potted houseplants together so that their leafy differences stand out. The impact comes from the diversity. Arrange and rearrange the combinations until you find one you like.

A ARROWHEAD VINE This variegated houseplant shares space with the thick, shiny oval succulent leaves of a jade plant.

B DRACAENA has spiky leaves that pair nicely with the puckery, rounded foliage of peperomia.

C PEPEROMIA offers color-swirled flat leaves that are versatile enough to contract with many other houseplants.

Portable Plants
Tropical Curtains

BEFORE

A Wall of Palms

TIME NEEDED
1/2 to 1
HOUR

Large containers filled with oversized plants can create a foliage diversion anywhere you need it.

AFTER
Think big when you shop for plants to shield a view. The fan-shaped waving leaves of a palm are the perfect diversion from the street traffic below.

What do you do when your patio—the relaxing space where you go to escape the world—overlooks a busy street and the top of the neighbor's garage? Simple. You create a view of your own. By pairing large containers with tall tropical plants, you can exchange an urban view for one that resembles a jungle treehouse.

A WALL OF PALMS

Thanks to the inexpensive cost and wide availability of large tropical plants such as parlor palms, you can buy a veritable jungle for very little cost. These plants grow very quickly and enjoy the hot summer weather. By using both short and tall versions of the same plant, you can create a wall of palm foliage that shields the view when you are sitting at a table as well as when you are standing.

MATCHING A POT TO A PLANT

When using tall, top-heavy plants such as palms, schefflera, or dieffenbachia, make sure that they are well grounded so they can survive a gust of wind. You can anchor them by planting in a heavy container made of terra-cotta, stone, concrete, or metal. If you're using a lightweight container, weigh down the plant/pot combo by adding bricks or stones to the bottom of the container before planting. If you are worried about protecting the floor on which the container will sit, use a waterproof saucer underneath the container. Use glazed clay or plastic saucers instead of terra-cotta; unglazed clay seeps moisture.

MAKING IT MOVABLE

Make your large plants mobile by placing their containers on wheeled bases before planting. Some rolling plant bases come with locking wheels to prevent them from moving around.

ALTERNATIVE CACHEPOTS

Think out of the box when it comes to choosing containers for large plants. Wicker laundry baskets, painted aluminum garbage cans, wastebaskets, or drainage pipes could make cool containers. An unusual container can transform a simple foliage plant into a fashion statement.

LARGE FOLIAGE PLANTS FOR SCREENING THE VIEW

NORFOLK ISLAND PINE
(ARAUCARIA HETEROPHYLLA)

BAMBOO PALM
(CHAMAEDOREA SEIFRIZII)

CROTON
(CODIAEUM VARIEGATUM)

TI PLANT
(CORDYLINE TERMINALIS)

MASS CANE
(DRACAENA FRAGRANS)

DUMB CANE
(DIEFFENBACHIA SPP.)

FALSE ARALIA
(SCHEFFLERA VEITCHII)

PONYTAIL PALM
(NOLINA RECURVATA)

FIDDLE-LEAF FIG
(FICUS LYRATA)

ENSURE PROPER DRAINAGE

1 LOOK FOR HOLES. Plants need ample drainage, or their roots may rot. Make sure all containers (whether planted or cachepots) have water drainage holes in the bottom.

2 DRILL FOR DRAINAGE. If a resin or terra-cotta container lacks holes or has small holes, use a drill with a masonry bit to create or enlarge them. Check the flow. Make the hole large enough for adequate drainage. To ensure even drainage, make several holes in the bottom.

Terra-cotta

Terra-cotta is a classic pot choice. It adds a subtle warmth to everything it contains and is widely available and fairly inexpensive. It comes in all sizes—from the smallest tabletop pots to large patio options.

Resin, Fiberglass, and Plastic

There are two big selling points to these manufactured pots—they are lightweight, and they come in a wide array of colors and textures. These compounds can mimic some of the most coveted heavier mediums.

STYLE CONSIDERATIONS The earthy good looks of terra-cotta are what attracts most container gardeners. It is an ideal choice if you are adding to your container collection over a period of time—because all terra-cotta more or less looks the same, it's easy to match. You can also find attractive terra-cotta pot feet that dress up any ordinary pot. In addition to adding a touch of interest or whimsy to the pot, they also lift the pot off the ground, which allows for more airflow—a healthier situation for both the pot and the plant.

DURABILITY Terra-cotta is available in two types—Italian and Mexican. It may be difficult to tell them apart; the differences are mainly in cost and durability. Terra-cotta made in Italy is fired at higher temperatures than Mexican terra-cotta, so it's denser and holds up to the elements better than the Mexican product. Overall, terra-cotta breaks easily—with Mexican terra-cotta being more fragile. Both types of terra-cotta are porous, so the plants that reside in them lose more soil moisture due to evaporation. And, if you live in a climate where it freezes in the winter, you will need to bring terra-cotta indoors to keep it from freezing and cracking.

COST FACTORS Terra-cotta is inexpensive. Mexican terra-cotta is less expensive, has a rougher texture, is more porous, and breaks more easily than Italian terra-cotta. Glazed terra-cotta usually costs more. As with most pots, large containers are more expensive.

STYLE CONSIDERATIONS Resin containers come in all colors, shapes, and sizes. From sleek modern pots to those that look like old-world classics, resin containers are the perfect option for gardeners who like to change styles every couple of years. They are also the ideal choice for large containers that may be planted with tender ornamentals such as citrus trees or jasmine because the big containers are lightweight enough to be moved easily, even when filled with plants and potting soil.

DURABILITY Resin, fiberglass, and plastic are created with durability in mind. They can take heat waves and freezes and still look great—therefore they are ideal for uses in all seasons. If dropped, they may crack or shatter, but on the whole they are much more durable than terra-cotta.

COST FACTORS Resin, fiberglass, and plastic containers are generally inexpensive choices.

OTHER TYPES OF POTS

CERAMIC POTS

Available in a rainbow of colors, ceramic pots are instant garden accessories for patios or tabletops. Used as cachepots, ceramic allows you to slip in any blooming plant from the garden center for an instant living bouquet. Keep cachepots of many sizes in your potting shed to accommodate the standard grower pot sizes. For a more finished look, top the drop-in plants with a layer of sphagnum peat moss (or any other attractive mulch option) to cover the black edges of the grower's pot for a more finished look.

Concrete

Cast concrete is the heaviest of all pot possibilities, with the exception of stone. Concrete is poured into molds of varying sizes, designs, and styles. Because of the weight, concrete cannot be moved easily to other locations.

Metal

Metal is the longest-lasting of all container types depending on the type of metal. These bottom-heavy containers are great for supporting top-heavy plantings such as small trees.

STYLE CONSIDERATIONS Concrete planters run the gamut from classical to modern. They can also be painted to match the color palette of any home's exterior. Touch-up painting may need to be done every several years.

DURABILITY Concrete is extremely durable and can take cold and heat extremes, so it's a good year-round container option.

COST FACTORS Concrete is less costly than stone, and depending on the manufacturer, it may cost less than resin pots.

STYLE CONSIDERATIONS Metal adds its own warmth, personality, and old-world elegance to any garden. Cast iron rusts to a natural brown, or it can be painted any color. Nonrusting zinc or aluminum make handsome silver-gray containers that look stunning with a wide range of colorful plantings. Copper offers orange-tinted hues until it ages to a greenish patina.

DURABILITY Metal containers are the most durable of all containers. Because metal containers are made from natural materials, rust and natural oxidation can change their outward appearance. Although many gardeners think that these natural processes enhance the look, the application of protective coatings will stop the aging.

COST FACTORS Aluminum containers are the least expensive of metal containers—and the lightest in weight. Cast iron, copper, and zinc are more costly than other types of containers but are also long-lived.

FOUND OBJECTS
Think creatively when it comes to containers. Old wooden boxes, desk drawers, watering cans, recycled coffee cans—all have the ability to show off plants in exciting and innovative ways. Drill holes in the bottoms of found-object containers to allow adequate drainage.

WOOD CONTAINERS
Usually made from weather-resistant cedar, wood containers offer a natural look. Treating wood containers with a preservative will make them last longer. When purchasing, check the joint construction, because wood shrinks and expands with moisture. To prevent wood rot, set containers on concrete or wood surfaces rather than on the lawn or ground.

DUAL-PURPOSE CONTAINERS
Home-improvement and office-supply stores offer a variety of containers that were originally made for other purposes but that can pull double duty in the garden. Mesh waste cans or wicker laundry baskets can be filled with sphagnum peat moss, potting soil, and both annual and perennial plants to create new twists.

Hanging Baskets

Be creative when hanging plants in your yard. Here, a well-established tree is the perfect (and natural) post for tiered plantings overflowing with impatiens.

Hanging baskets are the perfect way to create a flower-filled view. The lush flowers and foliage are like curtains of color.

For gardeners with more vertical than horizontal space, hanging plants are the perfect solution. And for gardeners who lack ground to garden—those who live in apartments, condos, or high-rises—hanging plants offer a way to garden without the benefit of terra firma.

A hanging basket is essentially an airborne garden. And while it may need more water that grounded gardens or containers (because it is more likely to lose moisture through evaporation), you care for a hanging basket the same way you do other containers.

HANGING OUT

Nothing says "home" like a traditional front porch lined with abundantly blooming hanging baskets. Flowering baskets are an instant impact solution to any less-than-romantic porch. With the simple addition of a screw-in hook (one strong enough to bear the weight of a fully planted—and watered—container), you can purchase or plant a lavish hanging garden that can be suspended in minutes.

BASKET BRAVADO

Other locations can benefit from the charms of a well-planted hanging basket. Try fitting the faces of fences or walls with brackets for hanging plants. Or suspend baskets from tree branches to dress up a low-impact area. These aerial gardens can even hang from the edges of a pergola or large arbor to add color where it is needed.

5 STEPS TO CREATE AWE-INSPIRING HANGING BASKETS

1 USE THE RIGHT SOIL.
Plants grown in containers, especially those in hanging baskets, require a lightweight potting soil mixture. Soil from your garden is too heavy. Potting mix also contains water-holding components, such as sphagnum peat moss, that will help prevent your plants from drying out.

2 MAKE SURE THE LIGHT IS RIGHT. Check the plant tags for light requirements, and group together plants with similar light requirements. Trailing annuals, such as petunias and geraniums, require

full sunlight. Shade-loving choices include ferns, ivies, and impatiens. It's also a good idea to pair plants that have the same water and plant food needs.

3 WATER, WATER, WATER. Hanging baskets are subject to the effects of wind and sun—more so than plants that live in the garden. They need watering every day, and if the weather is hot and dry, perhaps twice a day. Keep watering until water comes out of the container's drain holes.

4 CUT AND CLIP.
Cut off dead blooms and you'll encourage flowering annuals to produce more flowers. To keep plants from becoming leggy, clip back straggling tendrils.

5 FEED FOR FLOWER FLUSHES.
After planting, and every one or two weeks thereafter, spray baskets with a water-soluble plant food to keep foliage green and flowers blooming.

1 **2** **3**

HOW TO PLANT A HANGING BASKET

TIME NEEDED 1/2 to 1 HOUR

Lush, abundant hanging baskets are easy to make—you can assemble one in about a half hour. With a heavy-duty wire basket, a sturdy, water-holding liner, potting soil, and some eager-to-bloom plants, you can create a hanging wire basket as gorgeous as the ones you see in trendy garden stores and florists shops.

BUILD A BASKET OF BLOOMS

1 Start with six to eight trailing plants such as ivy geraniums or petunias.

2 Fill a hanging wire basket with a thick liner, such as moss or a fitted coco-fiber liner.

3 Fill the middle of the liner with potting soil and plant three or four plants as the "top tier" plantings. Plant the remaining plants in the bottom of the basket by poking them through to the soil.

Once you start hanging them up, it's hard to stop. Here, hanging plants transform a second-story terrace with a lush fringe of foliage and flowers.

Plant Plug-Ins

BEFORE

Changeable Landscapes

TIME NEEDED
1/2 to 1
HOUR

Transform a sparse border into a foliage and flower fantasy by dropping in blooming plants. This instant impact solution also allows you to change your garden's color scheme with little effort at a moment's notice.

AFTER!
By alternating the color pattern with dropped-in plants, you can make a border bolder and brighter. When the flowers fade, just pop out the spent plants and replace them with new ones.

DIRECTIONS

1 CUT OUT THE POT BOTTOM. Using a serrated knife with the blade positioned away from you, cut around and remove the base of the hanging pot to expose the plant's root mass.

2 REMOVE THE HANGERS. Use pliers to remove any wires attached to the pot.

3 DROP INTO POSITION. Dig a hole as wide and deep as the pot and drop the pot into the ground. Water well.

4 CHANGE OUT POTS. When you want to change color schemes or add a new flower to your border, simply lift the pot from the ground and replace it with a new one.

WHAT TO GET

MATERIALS
- 3 annual vinca (*Catharanthus roseus*) hanging baskets
- 3 begonia (*Begonia semperflorens*) hanging baskets
- Serrated garden knife
- Pliers

It's easy to fill in the blanks in a boring border when you buy big, bold, blooming plants and plug them in like missing puzzle pieces. All of a sudden they complete the whole picture—a sparse entryway becomes spectacularly welcoming.

DROP—AND POP!
Thanks to the wide availability of blooming annuals sold in large pots, homeowners have a colorful palette of plants from which to choose. And nothing jazzes up a monochromatic landscape faster than bold, bright color. It's easy too. Buy large blooming plants, preferably in large pots such as those sold as hanging baskets or in 1-gallon or larger containers. Then cut out the bottom of the pot, dig a hole, and drop the pot into the landscape. Pop! Instant impact color. The plants' roots are in touch with the soil below so they can take in water. And the plant can be fed from the top. But by planting this way—pot and all—it's easier than ever to pop plants out of the ground and replace them with another selection later in the season.

GO FOR COLOR
Color can carry a garden. Red and fuchsia flowers sizzle when paired with the plain green foliage of yew shrubs and hostas along a brick pathway (opposite). And it doesn't take a huge number of blooming plants to carry the color theme. By planting a blooming plant next to a foliage plant, you get the best contrast—and the most attention.

CHANGE YOUR SCHEME
Since these plants can be lifted easily from the ground, they can be replaced with new varieties to match your garden decorating whims. For example, if you are hosting a wedding or baby shower at your home, you can coordinate your entryway border flowers with the color theme of the party. Plus, this planting drop-and-pop method allows you to add seasonal flowers to your beds and borders. Pots of tulips look stunning in your spring garden, and once they fade, you can pop them out and replace them with a summer annual.

SEASONAL CHANGE-OUTS

Look for these plants, frequently sold in either large containers or hanging-basket containers, to drop into your garden.

SPRING
Tulip
Daffodil
Crocus
Pansy
Hydrangea
Lily
Campanula

SUMMER
Begonia
Daisy
Petunia
Fan flower
Million bells
Vinca
Verbena
Creeping zinnia
Impatiens
Water hyssop
Ivy geranium

FALL
Chrysanthemum
Aster
Kale
Holly
Ornamental grass

Window Boxes

A B
C D

Window boxes dress up the look of any house in a snap. And best of all, they create a wonderful view—from both inside the house and out.

Window boxes are the essential accessory items for the well-dressed house. Easy to purchase or build (it's just a box, after all), a window box gives you a great view from both inside the house and out.

You can use any type of plants for your window boxes. Although annuals are most common, perennials, small shrubs, and tiny trees can add instant seasonal color and structure to your window box—each for about the same price as a large annual. Here are some guidelines for choosing the plants for your window boxes.

MATCH YOUR HOME'S EXTERIOR TRIM

Think of the window box and its plantings as accessories for your home. The color of your home, and its trim, can help determine the color planting scheme of your window box. For example, baby blue house trim would look great with the azure blooms of fan flower planted near it. A house with green trim would be the perfect complement for an all-foliage window box of small cypress trees, ivy, and hosta. Cascades of white bubbling blooms can be achieved with water hyssop, white 'Wave' petunias, and cupflower.

ADD A NEW COLOR SCHEME TO YOUR YARD

Window boxes are the perfect way to introduce a new color theme to your yard. Choose a plant color palette (for example, pink) then accessorize your patio furnishings, containers, and awnings using the same and complementary colors to infuse a new color in your yard's scheme.

MIRROR A LOOK

Repetition is one of nature's style basics, and your window boxes can repeat a look your yard has already established. For example, if you have tall, columnar shrubs in your yard, repeat the look in your window box by choosing miniature versions or impostors such as Alberta spruce or cypress trees.

CREATE A NEW FEEL

Window boxes allow you to temper the look of your home. For example, if your house is angular and square, try an overflowing, gushing window box that softens the hard angles of the home. If your house is classic cottage style, you could plant more formal window boxes of boxwood and ivy to add an element of surprise.

WINDOW-BOX WONDERS

A PRETTY IN PINK
This sweet pastel window box is filled to the brim with two colors of impatiens. The soft-gray trailing string of hearts (*Ceropegia woodii*) offers vertical appeal too. Make sure to include plants that share sun and watering requirements in the window box so that they can all excel.

B ORANGE AID
Orange nasturtiums (with attractive speckled leaves) are the centerpiece of this window box. With its pansies and verbena, this colorful box also picks up the colors from the garden below—a great way to integrate a window box into an overall garden color scheme.

C COTTAGE GARDEN
A simple stone exterior is dressed up with a flower-and-foliage-filled window box—a country garden right outside the window. A mélange of cottage garden favorites, this window box includes ivies, coleus, daisies, and vinca.

D COUNTRY COLOR
This color-packed window box is vibrant with the vivid colors of classic red geraniums and purple verbena. The variegated grass adds height and a little taste of country to the window box. Sun-loving annuals are excellent long-blooming choices for window boxes.

Window Boxes
One Window Four Ways

Spring splendor

Summer sizzle

Fall festival

Four Seasons in a Box

TIME NEEDED
1 to 2 HOURS

Window boxes can change their looks each season. And when you keep consistent elements, seasonal changes are even easier.

SPRING SPLENDOR

Start the gardening season early with a wide variety of early-season plants that can take cold snaps. Pansy, viola, snapdragon, nemesia, sweet alyssum, dusty miller, ivy, primrose, and many perennial varieties (including spring bulbs you can transplant) thrive in cool temperatures. Some annuals, such as snapdragons and pansies, love cool weather best and shrivel as temperatures rise. Plant-buying tip: For instant impact color, buy plants already in bloom or heavily budded. At the garden center, use your cart as an impromptu window box to arrange the right mix of colors and textures.

SUMMER SIZZLE

Jazz up your spring window box with showy summer starters. Remove cool-weather spring flowers (pansies, bulbs) and replace them with plants that can take the heat—and actually relish it. These include trailing beauties such as 'Wave' petunias, licorice plant, sweet potato vine, and asparagus fern. Pack sunny window boxes full of both trailing and tall varieties. Plant them closer than you would in the garden for a more lush effect.

FALL FESTIVAL

An autumn window box can be a gorgeous assembly of some of the most colorful fall florals: mums in all colors; shades of blue and purple asters; and a wide variety of brightly flowering kale. These beauties are engineered to ride out the cool temperatures of autumn in style. Add gourds, miniature pumpkins, and Indian corn to window boxes for a fresh fall feel.

WINTER WONDER

Welcome winter with a window box that looks great whether frozen or snow-capped. Deck out your view with a winter motif using small-in-stature Alberta spruce (which will maintain its chartreuse green color all winter) and icicle plant (which may fail to overwinter in some climates but holds its icy white form). Add festive fun with stacked graduated terra-cotta pots that emulate Christmas trees. Dial up the color with red and green apples and pinecones.

WINDOW-BOX KNOW-HOW

1 USE LIGHTWEIGHT POTTING SOIL. A mixture with sphagnum peat moss is lighter than garden soil and has the ability to hold moisture—important in a window box that loses moisture fast.

2 HANG THE EMPTY WINDOW BOX, then fill it with soil and plant it. This sequence, while seemingly obvious, is important because hanging a soil-filled, planted box is difficult.

3 COMBINE PLANT TYPES. Plant both erect and hanging plant varieties to create a lush and varied look that fills both horizontal and vertical spaces.

4 PACK YOUR PLANTS TIGHTLY. It's not costly to fill the small space in a window box, and a mass of flowers creates the best effect.

5 BE A VIGILANT WATERER. Because window boxes are raised, they are often exposed to wind more than other container plantings. They may dry out faster than plants in other pots or in the ground, so be sure to water often.

6 FEED ONCE A MONTH during growth seasons. Annuals also benefit from occasional deadheading, which keeps blooms coming all season.

7 REMOVE AND REPLACE. If a plant fails to prosper in the window box or pull its weight in the overall effect, replace it with something flowering.

Winter wonder

EXPERT TIP Use small shrubs (such as Alberta spruce, Euonymus fortunei 'Emerald Gold,' and rounded miniature yew in window boxes as foundation plantings. They are often low-priced because they are so small. But in a window box, they take on a stature of their own. They add color and form, and fill in the box to make it look lush and beautiful.

Case Study
A Garden Party

PART
#1

AFTER!
Creating a flower-filled party zone in your yard is easy when you enlist plants, such as standard hibiscus, from other areas of the yard and garden.

SHOPPING LIST

GETTING THE LOOK

THE SEATING AND PLANTS
- 2 teak chairs
- 2 cushions
- 2 ottomans
- 4 planters
- 2 flats each of white and blue petunias
- 4 white hibiscus trees

THE SERVING AREAS
- Rain barrel
- Metal flower container
- 12 sheer curtain panels

THE LIGHTING
- 2 outdoor floor lamps
- Globe lamps
- Votive candles

Before

Create an outdoor room with all the comforts of home— soft, cozy cushions, comfy ottomans, and lamps that are wired for outdoor use.

A

B

C

Part One:
Alluring Ambience

TIME NEEDED
2 to 4 HOURS

Tick-tock—it's almost time for your big event. What can you do to your garden to make it an instant showcase? Roll up your sleeves to decorate your garden with style.

The garden is the perfect place to hold an afternoon tea, evening cocktail party, or special dinner with friends. With some instant impact staging, you can turn any outdoor area into the perfect place for a gathering.

GET READY TO PARTY

Having a party outdoors is similar to having one indoors— except you have more space. Hosting a party in your living room means vacuuming the rugs and cleaning up the clutter. Your yard requires the same sort of attention. From the lawn to the flowers to the shrubs, you need to straighten, nip, tuck, clip, and tidy your yard just as you would your home. The tips on page 59 will help you clean up your outdoor area.

ASSESS THE AREA

Determine where your party area will be and focus your energy there. Figure out where to place seating, how and where the food will be prepared and displayed, and the location of a well-stocked drinks station (especially if the weather will be hot). Once you've mapped out the party flow, so to speak, you can figure out the other aspects: flowers, lighting, and overall cleanup of the area.

IT'S PARTY TIME!

A CREATE A ROOM. The fastest way to contain a space is to hang sheer, floaty curtain panels. Battery-run globe lights help define the party's outer limits and offer a moonlike light source.

B USE GARDEN ACCENTS. Take the garden-party theme as far as you can by using actual items as serving pieces. An unused metal flower container is put into service when filled with ice to chill drinks.

C ROUND UP A SNACK STATION. A rain barrel dresses up for the evening by donning a top and tablecloth to become a snack station for hungry partyers.

Case Study
A Garden Party

PART
#2

Portable white-blooming double hibiscus trees, moved from elsewhere in the yard, create a small, friendly forest of flowering trees on the patio area.

Part Two:
Portable Plants

Moving pre-potted plants to the party area allows you to decorate quickly for any outdoor event.

When you prepare for a party indoors, you create bouquets and centerpieces. You can do something similar outdoors. Container plantings are the bouquets of an outdoor party. By bringing in pots of plants (made for the occasion, borrowed from other areas of your yard, or rented), you can decorate the party area with more than the natural surroundings. Portable plants can also support the party's color scheme or theme, and large potted plants are the perfect way to screen or block off private areas from guests.

Multiple serving stations in the garden encourage good party flow.

Grouping pots together creates an instant focal point.

A spare and colorless raised bed is brightened by a container of blooming verbena.

Part Three:
Night Lights

If your party is scheduled to continue after the sun has set, outdoor lighting is essential—both for safety and ambience. Light strands strung in the trees are a fast and festive way to provide overhead lighting. Torches or footed candelabra can be placed at the borders to delineate the party area. Water features with installed lighting beneath the surface add a warm glow to the night. If the party is in a remote area of the yard, a candlelit pathway can light the way. Another hint: Provide insect repellent for guests who are being bugged.

PART
#3

Battery-powered globe lights add ambience once the sun goes down. Other lighting options include floor-style lamps—wired for outdoor use—and twinkling votive candles.

Mow in advance

Rake your mulch

Water to green up

Spray down the patio

PREPPING FOR A PARTY

Getting ready for your outdoor party takes some planning. Here are things you should do before the big event.

MOW IN ADVANCE. If you like the newly shorn look of a recently mowed lawn, then you can wait until the day before the event to mow—but use a bagging attachment to keep your guests from tracking clippings into your porch, patio, and home. If you want a more verdant, but neat, look, mow two days before the event. Mowing the day of the event stirs up pollen, dust, and even insects. A one-day rest between mowing and the party allows everything to settle down.

MESS WITH YOUR MULCH. Using a rake, turn over your mulch to fluff it up a bit. If it is getting sparse (organic mulches such as cedar bark or cocoa bean hulls break down over time) or you like the look of a newly mulched area, apply a top layer of new mulch to spruce up the appearance.

WATER YOUR ENTRYWAY PLANTINGS. About an hour before your guests arrive, give the beds, borders, and containers around your entryway a good watering. It will give them a fresh lift so they look their best. Plus, large-leaved plants with glistening water droplets studding their leaves look like jewels in the garden.

SOAK YOUR LAWN. After a soft soaking rain, your lawn looks brilliantly lush and verdant. You can get the same look if you soak your lawn the day before your party. Soak the yard with about an inch of water to revive the green glow.

WASH OFF YOUR PATIO. Just before your guests arrive, hose down your patio bricks to remove dust and make them look clean and fresh. Wet patio pavers and bricks always look richer and more colorful after a bath. Blue stone or slate also takes on a darker, richer color. Even concrete looks more appealing when slightly wet.

CHAPTER THREE

PURE GARDEN THEATER

Creating an amazing garden space for an event just requires innovative thinking. Changing the landscape is more than a gardening feat—it can be a feat of magic.

In this chapter...

A B
C D

For your outdoor spaces to be truly enjoyed, they should mirror the elements of comfort and beauty that define your indoor spaces. The right furniture and outdoor accessories can make your patio and yard as livable as the inside of your home.

You can enjoy all the comforts of home in your own backyard when you outfit your outdoor living spaces with everything you need—seating, lighting, and all the accessories. Having the luxuries outdoors that you enjoy inside will ensure more use of your garden and yard.

PULL UP A SEAT

If you like to spend long hours in your garden sipping iced tea and reading the paper, comfortable seating is important. Although outdoor furniture is an essential element of garden design (a bench is a focal point in many gardens), it should also be comfortable. Sometimes, it may seem that the more durable outdoor furniture is, the less comfortable it is. Whether you choose teak, aluminum, wrought iron, or resin, comfort can often be as close as a cushion. Modern outdoor fabrics that are waterproof and eye-catching are also made to take the wear and tear that nature dishes out.

DINE ALFRESCO

If you like to dine outdoors, create an outdoor dining room space. You'll need a table large enough to serve your typical number of diners, as well as the appropriate number of chairs. Position the furniture in an area large enough to allow diners to sit comfortably. Outdoor dining areas also benefit from moving air—from an overhead or oscillating fan (the best way to ward off mosquitoes). Other dining-area comforts include washable table linens (tablecloths, placemats, and napkins), unbreakable plates and glasses, and candlelight (a candelabra adds a romantic touch).

ENTERTAINING AREAS

Think of outdoor entertaining areas in the same way you think about your den indoors. Organize so you have everything at your fingertips for ultimate comfort. Snacks and drinks can be brought out to the garden in wicker picnic hampers. You'll need serving surfaces, such as end tables and coffee tables. And cushions and fabric throws soften the edges of wooden or iron furniture.

COMFORT TOUCHES

A OUTDOOR ROOMS
Adding furniture to an area of your yard or garden creates an instant room out of unused space—a conversation niche, a place to read a book, a spot for afternoon tea. And decorative details enhance the space. Here, cushions top willow seating and a recycled log table to set the tone for a rustic retreat.

B LIGHTING FOR AMBIENCE AND SAFETY
Outdoor lighting comes in many forms—from simple candlelight to battery-powered or electric-wired options. Lighting options also provide a range of functions—from lighting pathways to offering instant nighttime ambience in the garden.

C SOOTHING SOUNDS
Sound in the garden enhances the experience of peacefulness. Flowing or bubbling water offers sounds that are both natural and soothing. Water gardens encompass a wide range of options, from inground pools to simple fountains.

D COMFORT WITHIN ARM'S REACH
Outfitting your outdoor spaces with all the comforts of home means paying attention to the details. Seating should be accompanied by end tables and other furniture that allows visitors to really kick back and relax. Here, a teak chaise has a pull-out table for drinks and a book.

Furniture and Props
Taking Indoors Out

For a special occasion, set your indoor furniture free in the great outdoors. Tea parties, alfresco dinners, or a child's birthday party—all take on the comforts of home when your indoor furniture comes out to play.

MOVING OUT

- Avoid leaving indoor furniture outdoors for more than a couple of days.

- Take in cushions or other stainable items when not in use.

- Protect furniture from rain, dew, wind, and sun.

- Avoid using electrical appliances anywhere near water.

An unused resin flower pot is the perfect height for an outdoor end table. Topped with plastic (better than glass for outdoor spaces), this end table provides space for drinks and snacks—all within arm's reach.

Moving your indoor furniture outdoors for an event seems somewhat irreverent. Your dining room table on the lawn, an overstuffed chair on the patio, a throw rug in the grass—the very placement seems to be breaking the rules. But there are no rules that say you can't enjoy the great outdoors in the comfort of your indoor furniture.

CHOOSE YOUR FURNITURE

The indoor furniture pieces that fare best outdoors are those that can take a little weather and wear—things like direct sunlight and errant golden retrievers jumping up for a look. For example, wooden tables and chairs for a dining area can be outdoors in good weather without being any worse for the wear. Leather couches or love seats are fun seating with the shag carpeting of a lush lawn underfoot. To protect furniture feet from the damp ground, set the furniture on tiles or bricks. But if kids and pets need to stay off the furniture indoors, those pieces are poor candidates for a trip outdoors.

THROW DOWN A RUG

Roll out a carpet to make a smooth walking surface. Make sure the ground beneath is even and free of lumps such as fallen nuts or tree branches. There are many brands of outdoor carpet that can remain outdoors all season. For prolonged use outdoors, keep carpets on concrete or wood rather than lawn areas.

HANG CURTAINS

To give the area a sense of scale and dimension, suspend curtain rods made from branches and hang sheer white panels, lace tablecloths, or brightly patterned shower curtains. Let them flutter in the breeze. Another curtain rod option—bamboo stakes from the garden.

MAKE YOUR BED

Imagine taking an afternoon nap with the cool breezes stirring around you. Move the daybed off the sunporch and into the yard for a perfect catnap. Suspend mosquito netting from a tree, position it around the bed, and take an afternoon nap in unbugged comfort.

ACCESSORIZE IN STYLE

Dress up a table in fine style: Cloth napkins are washable, fine silver is more or less weather-resistant, and fine china can be transported outside in a basket with handles. To make a formal "dining room," set the table near a tall hedge and hang a chandelier with lighted candles from an overhanging tree branch.

Few things are more inviting than a chaise in the garden. This four-poster outdoor nap spot is shielded from the sun by a rolled-out matchstick shade. Luxurious linens and pillows add a focal point to the verdant landscape.

Complete with dressing table and mirror, this outdoor bedroom has it all—everything but walls. Good indoor candidates for outdoor use are metal and heavy-duty rustic wood furniture.

Patio Four Ways
1. Tropical

 ## GETTING THE LOOK

FURNITURE

- Teak deck lounger
- 4 teak armchairs
- 36-inch-round teak table
- Umbrella

COLOR PALETTE

- Orange
- Yellow
- Blue
- Green

ACCESSORIES

- Color-themed buckets with yellow citronella candles
- Hanging paper globes
- Potted hibiscus

A Gloriosa daisy

B Hibiscus

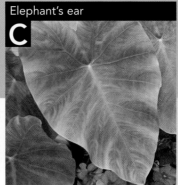

C Elephant's ear

D Coleus

Fantastic foliage, natural wood seating, and accessories in citrus-inspired colors deliver a tropical punch to your backyard patio or porch. Combine flashy foliage and lush, extravagant flowers in sizzling colors to create a tropical paradise anywhere—regardless of your garden's distance from the equator.

Exotic flowers and foliage, a canvas umbrella surrounded by classic teak furniture, and citrus-inspired accessories can transform any spot into a South Seas getaway.

TROPICAL PLANTS

To create a feeling of the tropics on any patio or porch, start with the showy, large-leaved plants that grow in that region. Umbrella-leaved banana and ample elephant's ear may be more likely to call places like Maui or Kauai home, but when you pot them in containers on patios and porches, these leafy beauties grow happily in summer's hot weather and can transform even the most austere location into paradise.

Bananas grow well in containers and will reach 10 to 15 feet tall. Plant them in the ground encircling a patio for a tropical punch. Another plus—their huge leaves can be harvested and used for tropical grilling dishes.

Elephant's ear, a tender bulb that produces huge leaves in the shape of an elephant's ear, grows vigorously in hot and humid weather. It, too, can be planted in the ground but must be lifted before freezing weather sets in.

You don't need tropical flowers to create a tropical feel. Gloriosa daisies are prairie natives, but they fit right into the theme with their citrusy colors. Many other annuals grow in tropical colors: impatiens, petunias, and lantana.

FUN FURNITURE

If you're looking for long-lasting outdoor furniture, then plantation-grown woods, such as teak, jarrah, and balau, are excellent choices.

To top off the theme, look to the colors and shapes of the jungle for advice. The colors of tropical fruits such as mango and papaya inspire accessories. Citrus-colored paper orbs hang like ripening fruit beneath the protection of a large white canvas umbrella. Candles burning from brightly colored buckets add a force field of citronella scent to discourage another tropical feature—the mosquito.

PLANT LIST

A GLORIOSA DAISY (*RUDBECKIA HIRTA* 'PRAIRIE SUN')
Golden petals surround a lime green center on this unusual gloriosa daisy. 'Prairie Sun' blooms on 3-foot stems from midsummer to frost. Plant gloriosa daisy in sun. A semihardy annual, it may reappear the following year.

B HIBISCUS (*HIBISCUS ROSA-SINENSIS*)
This tender tropical shrub will bloom all summer long, but it must be taken inside before frost in cold climates. The fantastic hand-size blooms have ruffly edges and long, elaborate stamens.

C ELEPHANT'S EAR (*COLOCASIA ESCULENTA*)
Commonly called elephant's ear for obvious reasons, colocasia leaves can grow up to 3 feet wide. Lovely fleshy leaves provide tropical drama when plants are in the ground or grown in containers. Dig these large, tropical bulbs in the fall, store in a cool, dry place over winter, and replant them each spring for years of showy effect.

D COLEUS (*SOLENOSTEMON SCUTTELARIOIDES*)
Easy to grow (and among the easiest plants to start from cuttings), coleus is a favorite shade-loving annual with new introductions tolerating sun as well. The foliage is the main event with this plant that sports wild splashes of color.

GETTING THE LOOK

FURNITURE

- 36-inch-round glass-topped table
- 2 metal mesh bar stools with arms
- Chiminea

COLOR PALETTE

- Burgundy
- Black
- Silver
- Green

ACCESSORIES

- 4 potted coleus plants
- 4 potted grass plants
- Standard hibiscus
- Small potted grass
- Martini bar set and glasses
- Red crystal vase
- Votive candle arch

Ducksfoot coleus **A**

Maiden grass **B**

Coleus **C**

Fountain grass **D**

Step outside into sleek sophistication with this cosmopolitan seating area. The black mesh table and chairs are surrounded by bright splashes of colorful coleus and architecturally appealing foliage fountains of ornamental grass. Every detail is perfect, down to the martini olives that complement the color scheme.

Plants are like chameleons—they reflect the style of their surroundings. Because of their flexibility, you can mix and match the plantings around your patio to reflect the look you want.

QUIET SOPHISTICATION
A cosmopolitan table and metal mesh chairs set the contemporary scene. The choice of high-style metal chairs upgrades the elegance of an outdoor setting. The subdued plant color palette, burgundy and green with hints of red, infuses the seating area with quiet sophistication.

COLOR AND TEXTURE
Color and texture are the starring elements in this patio setting. A ruby red vase is an instant centerpiece—just drop potted ornamental grass directly into the vase. The shape of the spiky grass centerpiece is echoed in the pots, containers, and ground plantings that surround the table. An arc of red votive candles on the table offers sparkling and sophisticated light for a memorable dining experience for two.

FANTASTIC FOLIAGE
Coleus, one of the most versatile foliage plants, offers color, texture, and varying leaf shapes—the perfect plant accessory in this sleek, modern seating area.

Standard hibiscus planted in pots at the edge of the patio offers floating orbs of vivid red blooms. Fountain grass, growing in pots, softens the edges around the patio seating area and displays joyous fountains of foliage.

AFTER HOURS
To extend the use of the patio into the chilly evenings of autumn, a metal chiminea sits at the patio's edge, ready to be lit for warmth and glow.

PLANT LIST

A DUCKSFOOT COLEUS (SOLENOSTEMON SCUTTELARIOIDES)
This unusual leaf form of coleus is a favorite among coleus aficionados. Named for its ducksfoot leaf shape, this coleus adds interesting color and shape. Coleus loves the shade but will take some sun. New sun-loving varieties of ducksfoot coleus include 'Indian Frills' and 'Purple.'

B MAIDEN GRASS (MISCANTHUS SINENSIS)
Tall and spiky, M. sinensis 'Gracillimus' is a clump-forming grass that looks great in all seasons. The narrow green leaves sway gently in the breeze. This grass, like most grasses, will grow in full sun or bright shade.

C COLEUS (SOLENOSTEMON SPP.)
Showy big-leaf coleus can fill a container or window box in just a season. Fast-growing and low-maintenance, coleus blooms at the end of the summer. The insignificant blooms can be pinched off to keep the lovely mounded shape of the plant. Popular varieties of burgundy and yellow coleus include 'Saturn' and 'Yin and Yang.'

D FOUNTAIN GRASS (PENNISETUM SPP.)
Pennisetums offer a wide range of adaptable and attractive grasses. Grown in pots or garden beds, they show graceful form and attractive seed-topped tips. P. alopecuroides 'Hameln,' also called dwarf fountain grass, is a clump-forming grass that can be grown in full sun to light shade.

3. Absolutely Asian

 SHOPPING LIST

GETTING THE LOOK

FURNITURE

- Molded resin couch with cushions
- Molded resin chair with cushion
- Molded resin coffee table
- 4 throw pillows

COLOR PALETTE

- Brown
- Green
- Black
- Cream

ACCESSORIES

- On-the-ground candles in ovals and orbs
- Watertight metal planters

Red-leaved banana A 	Horsetail B 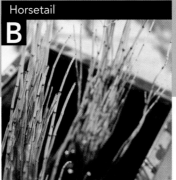	Flowering kale C 	Papyrus D 

Asian-inspired plantings and furnishings create an aura of Zen-like peacefulness on this patio. Molded resin bases and weather-impervious fabrics make this patio feel more like a living room than an outdoor space. Calming foliage plants of dramatic textures combined with neutral accessories make this look easy to emulate.

This Asian-inspired seating area pairs low and comfortable furnishings with exotic and textural plantings. The portable plantings, some in soil and some in water, allow a wide variety of plant foliage choices.

FUNCTIONAL FURNITURE

The weather-resistant resin wicker couch and chair are plumped for comfort with cushions covered with fabric that is also made to withstand the elements. The color palette—green, cream, brown, and black—is earthy and neutral, which helps create a quiet sense of serenity.

INFLUENCE OF WATER

Flanking the couch and chair are black metal containers filled with water and water-loving plants—horsetail and papyrus. To use metal or other containers for small, impromptu water gardens, line the interior of the container with black plastic. To read more about creating water gardens, see pages 88–91 and page 99.

TALL TROPICALS

Tall-standing banana and pots of spiky grass add texture, rather than color, to the seating area. The subdued, frilly foliage of a potted flowering kale is this scene's only flash of color. The plants are selected for their textural participation rather than for their color—a design tenet of Asian style.

NIGHT LIGHTING

On-the-ground candles, made entirely out of wax, create a luminous glow when lit; when unlit, they add organic form to the setting.

The trio of tabletop candles (covered with a reedy exterior material) echoes the reedlike texture of the equisetum spikes in the black container water gardens.

Simplicity of form—all of it functional—makes this seating area calm, relaxing, and in sync with an evening spent with friends.

PLANT LIST

A RED-LEAVED BANANA (ENSETE VENTRICOSUM)
Ornamental bananas grow well in pot culture and offer height and form to patios and porches. From a single elegant stem, long leaves unfold like an umbrella. Bananas love hot weather and full sun. Plants grow up to 10 feet tall in a single season.

B HORSETAIL (EQUISETUM SPP)
This attractive plant was around when the dinosaurs roamed the earth. Horsetail grows in moist, sandy soil or in a container set directly in shallow water. The elegant hollow reeds grow up to 3 feet tall. There are dwarf varieties of horsetail that are great water garden plants.

C FLOWERING KALE (BRASSICA OLERACEA)
Looking more like a floral bouquet than a vegetable, flowering kale offers colorful frilly leaves and a hardy disposition. Great for containers or window boxes, flowering kale is a long-lasting plant in the fall garden. This annual stands up to light frosts.

D PAPYRUS (CYPERUS PAPYRUS)
Water-loving papyrus sends up tall stems topped with a whirligig of foliage. Papyrus, a sedge, must be planted in pots and submerged in water. It prefers full sunlight and can grow from one to fifteen feet tall, depending on the species.

71

Patio Four Ways
4. Totally Traditional

GETTING THE LOOK

FURNITURE

- Black wrought-iron table
- 4 black wrought-iron arm chairs
- Umbrella and umbrella stand

COLOR PALETTE

- Yellow
- White
- Black
- Green

ACCESSORIES

- 2 pots of rosemary
- 2 pots of scented geranium
- 2 topiary eugenia
- 2 privet hedges in pots
- Pot of yellow lantana
- Ficus tree
- Pot of gloriosa daisy
- Country tabletop ceramic dishware
- Bouquet of fresh-cut 'Teddy Bear' sunflowers

Privet

A

Eugenia

B

Lantana

C

Scented geranium

D

This trendy twist on the traditional marries the formality of topiary and lattice planters with French country tabletop accessories. The result is pure classic comfort.

Traditionally inspired gardens have been the outdoor trendsetters for the last century. But traditional is anything but old and stuffy. Far from it: Traditional can be as relaxed and flower-filled as you make it. Classic in design, a traditional garden is in fashion now, and it will be 10 years from now because traditional is timeless.

CLASSIC SEATING

The classic furniture of this patio dining area includes lattice-backed wrought-iron table and chairs. The umbrella stand adds a decorative flourish of style while it supports a simple white canvas umbrella, which allows patio partyers to enjoy a meal without the glare of sun or sprinkle of rain.

THE PALETTE OF THE SUN

The color palette reflects the colors of a sunny Provençal landscape—white, yellow, and restful green. The sunny French country tabletop accents include rustic bowls and plates with sunflower yellow cups. A bouquet of 'Teddy Bear' sunflowers nods casually to the traditional plants that surround the table. Finely clipped balled topiaries of eugenia flank the dining area. Pots of yellow-blooming gloriosa daisies and lantana dot the area with flashes of warm color. And to create a sense of structure and privacy for the patio dining area, large potted privets stand sentry.

SCENT-SATIONAL CONTAINERS

Because dining is such a sensory experience, the area is filled with the scents and tastes of the garden. Pots of cone-shaped rosemary sit close at hand to allow diners to snip fresh herbs to season savory salads and hearty soups. Scented geraniums in pots also add a fragrant touch.

PLANT LIST

A PRIVET
(LIGUSTRUM VULGARE)
A hardy shrub, privet is a favorite hedge planting. Covered with small green, glossy almond-shaped leaves from spring to fall, it also produces small white fragrant flowers in early spring. This fast-growing shrub makes an excellent privacy screen or living fence because of its branching density. It grows 4 to 15 feet tall.

B EUGENIA
(EUGENIA MYRTIFOLIA)
Eugenia myrtifolia is a subtropical evergreen that adapts well to topiary forms. In spring eugenia bears small white flowers. In cold climates, it can be kept indoors. To keep a neat globular form for topiaries, clip off new growth several times a year.

C LANTANA
(LANTANA CAMARA)
Available in a wide range of colors (some varieties sport multicolored flowers), lantana is an annual in colder climates but a perennial in warmer climates. It has woody stems with small rough-coated leaves. Its rangy growth habit makes it attractive in containers and window boxes.

D SCENTED GERANIUM
(PELARGONIUM FRAGRANS)
Rub the leaves of this amazing herb and you'll release a marvelous scent. Scented geraniums come in a huge range of fragrances, including mint, chocolate, citrus, and rose. They have small, insignificant blooms—so the major appeal of scented geraniums is their fragrance.

At a Glance: Outdoor Furniture

Teak

Long-lasting tropical woods, such as teak, provide classic looks and extreme longevity. Teak is a heavy-duty wood used by shipbuilders.

Aluminum

Aluminum furniture is sporting new, exciting looks. This chair, created to look like a woven material, provides weatherproof durability and stylish good looks.

STYLE CONSIDERATIONS Although teak is a typical choice for traditionally inspired furniture, it is also used to make contemporary, modern, and Mission-style outdoor furniture. From steamer chairs to end tables, teak is the wood of choice for many homeowners who want long-lasting furniture. Teak also adapts to the look of any garden style. A teak Luytens bench sitting at the end of a pebble path in a traditional boxwood-edged garden looks as much at home as a teak curved-back bench in a country garden.

DURABILITY If you're looking for long-lasting outdoor furniture, plantation-grown woods, such as teak, are the way to go. Teak, a wood that sailing ships are made from, is exceptionally strong and resistant to decay. Over time, its honey-colored wood weathers to a silvery gray when left outdoors. Durable enough to overwinter in the most challenging climates, teak furniture can easily last for decades.

COST FACTORS Teak is the most costly but also the most long-lasting of the outdoor furniture materials.

STYLE CONSIDERATIONS Aluminum furniture is lightweight and available in many different styles. There are two types of aluminum: extruded and cast. Extruded-aluminum frames usually feature tubular forms and sling or strap seats. These easy-to-lift pieces are mobile, and the chairs can be stacked if tight winter storage is a consideration. Cast aluminum weighs more and features more intricate design options than extruded aluminum.

DURABILITY Because it doesn't rust or wear, aluminum is durable and long-lasting. Both types of aluminum are fairly maintenance-free because they are sealed with durable powder-coated finishes.

COST FACTORS Aluminum furniture comes in a range of prices. Depending on the style and brand, it can be as expensive as wood furniture.

OTHER TYPES OF FURNITURE

RESIN A popular and inexpensive choice for outdoor entertaining areas, resin furniture is lightweight, easy to move, and uniform in size, which means it's stackable and easily stored.

Resin is easy to care for and durable. A hard spray with the hose in the spring generally is all the cleaning required. For more stubborn dirt or marks, use dishwashing liquid and a soft brush to clean up.

All-Weather Wicker

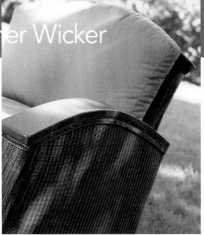

Wicker was once used only on protected front porches and in screened rooms, but new all-weather wicker can go outside and stay there.

STYLE CONSIDERATIONS Wicker can infuse a porch or patio with a comfortable and old-fashioned look. Bold colors and contemporary styling can also make wicker a contender with other design schemes. New, improved outdoor wicker can be used anywhere in the yard because it's made to take extremes of weather.

DURABILITY As durable as metal but without the weight and possible rust problems, new outdoor wicker looks like furniture you might put in your living room.

COST FACTORS Designer wicker can be expensive, but its durability makes it a good long-term investment.

Cast Iron

Cast iron is available in many designs and colors—from Victorian frilly to cool contemporary. It offers long-lasting, hardworking, and beautiful seating options.

STYLE CONSIDERATIONS Cast- and wrought-iron furniture is available in a wide range of styles and colors. Heavy-duty, durable, and attractive, cast iron is a good choice for areas that receive a lot of wind because it is the heaviest of all furniture.

DURABILITY While iron can rust over time, many manufacturers use finishes that protect the metal against weathering. Cast-iron furniture should last for decades with regular use.

COST FACTORS Iron furniture is costly, but like all-weather wicker, its cost needs to be weighed against its expected longevity.

SOFTWOODS

Softwoods, such as cedar and pine, are widely available in furniture. Unfortunately, softwoods have a much shorter life outdoors than hardwoods.

Prices of wood furniture vary with the longevity of the wood, with the longest-lasting hardwoods bearing the heftiest price tags.

Give softwoods longer lives by placing them on dry ground. Keep wood pieces from direct contact with soil or lawn.

You can also increase the longevity of wood by treating it with a sealant to defeat weathering color changes and maintain the wood's natural color. Occasional cleaning with soap and water chases most soil away. To remove mildew on pine furniture, use a bathroom cleaning product designed to eliminate mildew.

Magic with Paint

A B
C D

Paint—it's the ultimate instant impact medium. Brush or spray it on to cover a multitude of sins or to change your garden's color scheme at a moment's notice.

The structures in your garden—walls, arbors, furniture, fences, decks, gates, even pots—all offer a canvas for infinite color possibilities. Paint can create a masterpiece out of a structure you wouldn't think twice about. For example, think about the famous water-lily paintings by Impressionist painter Claude Monet. When he painted a simple arched bridge over an inlet in his water garden, this green-blue bridge, reflected in the water lily flower-studded pond, showed the entire world how a painted structure in a landscape adds elegance.

Using color by the gallon is creative and easy. The best thing about it is that if you grow tired of the color or change garden themes, you can brush on a new coat of paint in another color.

COLOR CONCEPTS

Color is one of the predominant themes in a garden. Creative flower and foliage combinations are exciting to gardeners. But there is color beyond the petal and leaf that can make a big impact in the garden. Painted color can create a backdrop or a theme when used in the right ways. For example, painting a wall in your garden a bold color can allow you to plant fewer plants—or at least less flamboyant ones. Color can also be used as an element of continuity in the garden, appearing in one place, such as a purple arbor, and then repeating on a pot or window box in the same purple hue.

THE BIG SPLASH

A garden can be influenced by the paint colors that you choose and the structures that are painted. Hot colors, such as fuchsia, red, yellow, and orange, dominate and should be used either sparingly or for dramatic effect. Cool colors, such as blue, green, and pastels, are recessive and can be used more readily. Painting a willow plant support or an arbor allows you to enhance an already dramatic focal point. And the plant pairing possibilities with painted structures open a whole new world of color coordination.

COLOR CONTINUITY

Color in the garden is often bold, but it also can quietly participate in the overall garden drama in substantial but subtle ways. For example, two common paint pairings are green and white. Classic and understated, green-and-white painted objects blend into the garden. Green doesn't compete for attention with flowers, and in fact is the perfect foil for flower brilliance. White-painted objects seem to glow in predominantly green backgrounds and add a crisp cleanliness to a garden.

BRUSH-ON COLOR

A ACCENT AND ARCHITECTURE

The versatility of paint allows you to change the accent color of your garden at your whim. Here, a purple arbor, plant pedestal, and fence set the stage for drama in the garden. Color-coordinating plant colors with plantings is a great way to make a dramatic statement in the garden. And the best thing about paint is that you can change the color scheme anytime you want.

B WALLS AND FENCES

Nothing imposes color faster in a garden than painting a wall or fence a wild color. Here, a pool area and container garden sizzle with a hot-pink wall as a backdrop. Using paint to cover a large area draws attention to it in a bold way.

C FESTIVE FURNITURE

Even the most modest of furniture, the classic picnic table, takes on a racy feel when painted fire engine red. You can recycle old furniture for new outdoor use by painting it fun colors. The paint also helps preserve the life of softwoods such as pine.

D FLASHY FLOORING

Decking or concrete flooring instantly gets a new life with a fresh coat of paint. Special flooring paints are made to withstand repeated foot traffic and furniture placement. Stains are also available, in a wider range of colors than ever before.

Magic with Paint
Inexpensive Furniture

AFTER!

Yikes, stripes! Resin takes on a whole new personality when painted with bright colors.

GETTING THE LOOK

SHOPPING LIST

MATERIALS

- Plastic spray paint
- Good-quality artist's brushes in flat and round shapes
- Cleaner (depending on the condition of the furniture)

Freshen Up Plastic Outdoor Furniture

Thanks to colorful new paints specifically made to cover plastic effectively, inexpensive outdoor furniture gets a new chance at life.

TIME NEEDED 2 to 4 HOURS

With plastic outdoor furniture available nearly everywhere—at amazingly low prices—it's hard to pass up these ubiquitous tables and chairs of summer. Inexpensive as well as convenient, most stack and store away for the winter with ease. The only downside of these outdoor furnishings is their color. Most are produced in white and the occasional green. Previously, if you wanted color, you needed to look elsewhere. Until now.

Paints created specifically to bond to plastic offer new, colorful looks. These special paints offer a wide range of colors, letting you create your own custom furniture designs. With a base coat and some creative freehand brushstrokes, you can transform a basic, unassuming white table into a swanky striped drink station in a couple of hours.

1 BEFORE

2

3

4

1 START WITH A CLEAN CANVAS. The benefits of plastic outdoor furniture are that it is widely available and inexpensive. But, if basic white is too tame a color scheme for your garden, then dress up chairs and tables with a funky coat of paint.

2 REMOVE LOOSE PARTICLES AND DIRT. If you are painting new or unweathered objects, wipe surfaces with a standard paint thinner. For aged or weathered objects, wipe surfaces with an ammonia-based cleaner. (Apply the liquid to the wiping cloth, not the furniture.)

3 APPLY A BASE COAT. Hold the spray-paint can 8 to 10 inches from the surface and spray with a sweeping motion. Overlap each pass by about a third. Apply multiple light coats to avoid paint runs and drips. Depending on the color, you may have to apply six or more light coats. Additional coats can be applied every 30 seconds.

4 ADD STRIPES. You can mask the dry surface and spray additional colors over the base coat. Or you can use brush-on paint to create other shapes, flowers, or unique designs. Let the paint dry before applying a new color.

TRANSFORMING METAL STRUCTURES WITH PAINT

Painted metal garden accents look great when they are brand-new, but pretty soon the elements change their appearance. Rather than put up with the look of rust, you can take some simple steps to turn back the ravages of time and weather.

PUT THE BRAKES ON RUST. Remove rust spots with fine-grade steel wool. If the spots refuse to come up easily, add a small dab of kerosene or commercial rust remover. Deep scratches and peeling paint can be removed with a wire brush or fine-grade sandpaper.

TOUCH UP OR RECOLOR. With the rust removed, you can add touch-up paint to restore a like-new appearance. Or you can spray-paint the surface and change the object's color entirely. Spray the surface with two coats of a rust-resistant primer, followed by a final coat of color.

KEEP IT BRIGHT. Coat your painted wrought iron with car wax to keep the paint bright and weather-safe.

Magic with Paint
All Decked Out

It takes minimal time and money to transform your deck from sorry to spectacular.

TIME NEEDED
6 to 8
HOURS

Look out your patio doors. You may find your deck is a lackluster, flat, planked area between your house and yard. A quick-and-easy makeover could turn it into a destination rather than a disappointment. Decking can rise above the ho-hum. An infusion of color is sometimes all it takes to transform an underused spot into a place where you look forward to spending time.

Older decks especially need an updated look. And with a wide variety of stain options, you can effectively change the look of your deck in a few hours. All without lifting a saw.

GO FROM DRAB TO DASHING

Wood stains come in a wide array of cool colors. They create a great basis for your deck's color theme. Follow through the color coordination with colorful furniture (or cushions), flowerpots, and plantings. Using two or more stain colors opens even more design possibilities. Adding small decorative touches such as post caps, wood trim, and lighting gives instant impact style. Next, outfit your deck with all the comforts of a great den. Add speakers for music and cushions for comfort. You can even extend the time you use your deck by adding heating options (propane heaters or wood-burning outdoor fireplaces) or cooling options (ceiling fans or overhead water misters).

BEFORE

SHOPPING LIST

GETTING THE LOOK

MATERIALS

- Gloves
- Safety glasses
- Broom
- Power washer
- Drop cloth
- Sanding sponge
- Roller and extension pole
- Deck color stain
- Pump sprayer (optional)

Cracked boards may need to be replaced or sanded before you paint the decking.

AFTER!
A painted pattern on the floor emulates the look of a throw rug. Two-toned decking rails offer climbing space for vining plants.

SELECT THE RIGHT STAIN

A wide variety of stain choices will help you achieve different looks. Here are your options:

CLEAR STAINS allow the beauty of the natural wood grain to shine through.

TONERS highlight wood grain, provide protection, and add a hint of color.

SEMITRANSPARENT STAINS provide rich, pigmented color that still allows the natural wood grain to show.

1 INSPECT DECK THOROUGHLY. Check for loose spindles, rotting decking planks, and loose nails. Make repairs.

2 WASH IT. Once the deck is structurally fit, wash all surfaces that will receive a coat of stain. If there are rough areas, sand lightly to make smooth. You can rent a power washer to make the cleanup go faster.

3 APPLY STAIN ACCORDING TO MANUFACTURER'S INSTRUCTIONS. Select hues that match your home's exterior or your deck's established color theme. Here, easy-to-roll-on blue and green stains create a simple four-square pattern—almost like a painted-on throw rug—providing a clear, decorative deck focal point. The rest of the deck is painted with a lighter blue stain. Both blues are repeated in the railing to connect the floor colors with the entire deck structure.

4 ALLOW THE STAIN TO DRY OVERNIGHT. Then place furniture, plants, and other decorative items.

Fantastic Fabric

A B
C D

Folds of fabric offer every color in the rainbow for your garden's immediate transformation—canopies, tents, privacy screens, banners, tablecloths, and more.

Fabric offers a world of instant impact possibility for your yard and garden. Tablecloths, shower curtains, sheer curtain panels, and plain-and-uncut fabric off the bolt all have the ability to transform your yard—by the yard. Turn a front porch into a secret hideaway with the simple addition of cheery curtains. Suspend yards of see-through netting from a tree and allow it to cascade and settle on the ground around an outdoor seating area, and you've created an exotic Moroccan locale. Fabric offers infinite instant impact options when it comes to defining space, creating backdrops, and adding color.

FLUTTERING WALLS

In the great outdoors of your backyard, building walls

requires time and money; plus, they're permanent—unless they're made of fabric. Creating the illusion of a wall by enclosing an area with fabric is easy. Even though your walls may flutter in the breeze (which has its own appeal), these temporary walls delineate an area in your yard and create the illusion of defined space. Fabric is wonderfully fluid and can be hung or draped from almost anything. Use natural "curtain rods" such as bamboo stakes, tree branches, or appropriate lengths of copper tubing from plumbing supply departments at home improvement stores. For entire room enclosures, wrap a wire gazebo, à la artists Christo and Jeanne-Claude, with the fabric of your choice.

BROCADE BACKDROPS

You can create fabric backdrops to cover or block out unsightly areas. It's called creatively directing the eye. Drape a paint-peeled garage side with a swath of fabric to disguise what you may someday get around to painting. Fabric has even more uses than paint because you can toss it up and pull it down quickly. You can try new looks and changeable color schemes, some of which may inspire you to create more permanent changes in your garden.

FABRIC FUN

A PERGOLA PICKUP
Striped awning cloth suspended from a pergola adds a sense of festivity to the structure. You can use any type of fabric for an evening or two, but for long-term use, opt for weather- and sun-resistant materials.

B DECKED OUT DINING
Fun party fabric dresses up an outdoor dining experience. Here, a simple rectangle of cloth creates a ceiling under which to dine. Netting-swathed deck chairs take on an ethereal, floating aura. A print tablecloth adds just the right amount of color to this woodland feast.

C TEMP TENTS
Erecting a tent for any event enhances the festivity—it's why circuses use them! Set up a temporary tent with simple fabric and decorative dowels. String guy supports will keep it in place for your afternoon party—offering a shaded spot for a cool repast.

D MOROCCAN MEAL
Flowing yellow fabric strung from a tree creates the space for a Moroccan meal alfresco. The natural folds and flow of fabric allow you to create intimate areas by partitioning them off with cloth.

Fantastic Fabric
Bold Barriers

Flags and banners add both color and movement to your landscape. Simple triangles of fabric, fluttering from the tops of poles inserted into your lawn—like oversized and flamboyant golf flags—add color and whimsy to your landscape. Flags can be homemade or purchased with a colorful welcome message.

TABLECLOTHS AND CUSHIONS

Tablecloths and cushions on outdoor furniture can change the entire mood of a garden setting. Besides making wooden or metal furniture more comfortable, cushions allow you to change the look by introducing color. Bold primary colors can complement plantings. Stripes instill nautical crispness into even the most land-locked locations. And flowered chintz prints can transform a simple table and chairs into a seating spot worthy of a formal tea.

LEFT Airy fabric transforms a basic table and chairs into a perky party setup. ABOVE RIGHT Make a party streamer from oilcloth triangles sewn onto a ribbon.

WEATHERPROOF FABRICS

For long-term outdoor use, buy fabric that can stand up to the elements. Nautical supply stores offer a wide range of weather-resistant fabrics. Available in many solids and stripes, they can help you add a crisp, long-lasting look to outdoor decor with no-fade awnings and upholstery fabrics. Nautical supply stores are also great places to find steel and brass fittings that can be used to lash down shades and awnings to make them more stationary in the wind. Other outdoor textiles include oilcloth, which can be cut to fit or sewn, as well as printed acrylic that's available by the yard.

Striped Privacy Screen

Create your own private area by making a movable screen with fabric and shepherds hook plant hangers.

GETTING THE LOOK

SHOPPING LIST

MATERIALS

- 4 yards of 54-inch-wide weatherproof striped fabric
- Thread
- 16 extra-large eyelets (1 extra-large $^7/_{16}$-inch)
- Eyelet kit, which includes a tool and 10 eyelet sets, and 1 extra-large eyelet refill
- 12 loose-leaf binder rings
- 4 sturdy cast-iron double shepherds hooks with three-prong footing

DIRECTIONS

1 ROLL IT OUT. The screen is one continuous piece of fabric, so no cutting is necessary. Turn the fabric so the stripe pattern is horizontal. Trim the selvage and stitch a hem along the top and bottom (long sides) of the fabric. Allow 2 inches of fabric at each short end for a hem. Double roll and stitch a hem at each short end. Stitch a one-inch band on the back side of the fabric to divide the fabric into three equal-size sections (and to create an area to place eyelets).

2 ADD THE EYELETS. Following the manufacturer's instructions on the eyelet package, attach four extra-large eyelets down each end of the fabric and down each band on the fabric, attaching a total of 16 extra-large eyelets. Cut and stitch four 24-inch-long fabric ties.

3 HANG IT UP. Push the four shepherds hooks into the ground at about 3-foot intervals. Insert the fabric ties through the four eyelet holes across the top of the fabric. Insert the 12 binder rings in the remaining 12 eyelet holes. Attach the ties and binder rings to the shepherds hooks. At the ends of the screen, hang baskets of plants on the shepherds hooks for a final flourish.

Fun with Lattice

Lattice is to garden walls what curtains are to windows. In other words, you can conjure a classic coverup with some well-placed lattice.

TIME NEEDED
1 to 2 HOURS

Light, airy, lacy—lattice panels allow you to create free-floating walls of privacy throughout your landscape. With them, you can screen out neighbors, shield yourself from street traffic, or hide an unattractive view. Lattice panels provide an instant, good-looking, and inexpensive barrier to unwanted views. Available in a variety of panel sizes at any home improvement store, lattice can be cut to fit almost any space. In addition to classic crisp white lattice, these versatile panels come in other colors. They can also be painted to match any outdoor decor. Whether you select wood or vinyl, lattice panel screens instantly improve the look of your patio.

PERMANENT OR TEMPORARY SCREENS

The versatility of lattice panels allows you to use them in a variety of ways. Hanging from the edges of a pergola, lattice panels give instant vertical definition to a seating area. An undefined patio area becomes an outdoor room with the simple addition of hanging (and removable) walls.

ABOVE Two same-size rectangular panels create an airy and open wall as a backdrop to an outdoor seating area. **CENTER** Chains hold the lattice panels in position. In windy areas, you may want to secure the panels from the base as well. **BOTTOM** The airy space is accentuated by the fact that the lattice panels float above the ground.

VINYL VS. WOOD LATTICE—HOW THEY STACK UP

VINYL LATTICE PANELS
Never need painting
One-piece construction
Can be nailed, screwed, and cut like wood
Solid color throughout
Termite proof
Decay proof

WOOD LATTICE PANELS
Can be nailed, screwed, and cut
Paintable
Constructed with rust-proof galvanized staples
Termite resistant
Decay resistant

FENCING. Lattice offers instant impact as fencing material. Panels can be mounted between decorative posts to create movable or permanent walls.

WALL REVIVAL. Screw lattice panels into concrete or wooden walls to create a finished facade that also gives climbing plants a foothold to scramble upward.

FOLDING SCREENS. Three rectangular lattice panels, hinged together, create a screen that you can move from location to location in the garden or on the patio.

DECORATIVE DISGUISES. Cracking foundations, crawl spaces, and a variety of other structurally important but unattractive places in your yard can be effectively disguised with lattice panels.

BEFORE

TIME NEEDED
2 to 4 HOURS

AFTER!

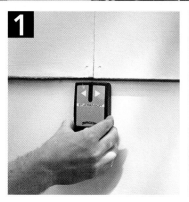
1

2

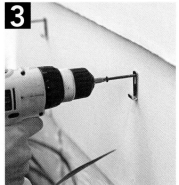
3

4

MIRROR AND LATTICE PANELS

Make any small garden look bigger by adding a mirror to reflect the surroundings. By placing lattice over the mirror, you create a lovely wall that can also support climbing vines.

1 FIND A STUD. Using a stud finder, locate the stud so that you can screw the lattice into a firm support.

2 MEASURE FOR LEVEL PLACEMENT. Use a level to mark the top position of the lattice panel.

3 ADD MIRROR HOOKS. Position the mirror hooks to the side of the building. Hang the mirror.

4 AFFIX THE LATTICE. Position the lattice over the mirror. Using a power drill and screws, attach the lattice to the side of the building. Avoid drilling into the mirror.

Magic with Water

A B
C D

Water gardens are the perfect meditative garden accessory. The best news is that even in a small space you can reap all of their relaxation benefits.

Tabletop water fountains, fountains that hang on the wall, and even small containers can provide all of the important essentials of a full-fledged water garden. They offer water, of course, floating and grounded plants, fish and other aquatic creatures, and a fountain or pump that provides both movement and sound. A water garden can be assembled quickly, so you can start enjoying the wonders of water the same afternoon you put it together.

WATER GARDEN VESSELS

Large or small, any container—wood, terra-cotta, stone, metal or a woven basket—can hold a water garden, as plastic liners allow you to make any vessel watertight. Crocks and metal containers such as washtubs, buckets, feed pails, and livestock troughs also make eye-catching water gardens. The vessels don't even need to be watertight; a simple plastic liner or a water sealant will stop any leaking.

FLOATING WATER PLANTS

Water gardens allow you to garden in an entirely different way. There are several types of plants that float languidly on the surface of any freshwater source. Two attractive floating plants that will thrive in even the smallest water gardens are water hyacinth *(Eichhornia crassipes)* and water lettuce *(Pistia stratoites)*. Both of these floating plant species can be extremely invasive in open waterways, so compost them at the end of the summer.

Even small water gardens can support water lilies. Planted in a submerged container, these flat-leaved water plants are beautiful, calming, and easy to grow. Miniature hardy water lilies that excel in container water gardens (needing at least 3 to 5 gallons of water) include yellow-flowering *Nymphaea tetragona* 'Helvola' (yellow), *N. × laydekeri* 'Fulgens' (red), and *N.* 'White Laydekeri' (white).

FISH AND OTHER AQUATIC FEATURES

It's a thing of beauty to watch a long-finned goldfish swishing its way around a water garden; it is also a necessity. Fish and snails are the cleanup crew of any water garden, eating algae and mosquito larvae that breed in open fresh water. Koi are too big for small water gardens, but they can be kept in larger ponds.

TAKE THE DIVE

A BARREL WATER GARDEN
You can transform any found vessel into a life-filled water ecosystem with a few considerations. The container must be watertight (add a plastic liner if necessary). Petite water lilies such as 'Helvola' are perfect fits for miniature water gardens. Small koi or goldfish add color and movement and gobble up mosquito larvae too.

B MILLSTONE FOUNTAIN
The sound of bubbling water in your garden is both restful and invigorating. A rustic fountain made of stacked millstones forms a gurgling focal point for a country garden.

C MODERN APPEAL
Stacked concrete squares sprout a gentle stream of tumbling water. Plumbed with a pump set, this attractive modern fountain would be at home in a large garden or small courtyard. You can make a fountain out of almost anything, using commercially available pump sets.

D THE ZEN OF WATER
Water is a key element in Japanese gardens. The flow, movement, and sound all contribute the important elements of water. A bamboo fountain adds small but continuous trickling sounds and adds movement to the garden.

Magic with Water
Afternoon Delight

If you liked playing with blocks as a kid, you'll love this easy-to-construct water garden feature—complete with plants, fish, and a waterfall.

TIME NEEDED
4 to 6 HOURS

If you are yearning for the soft sounds of water in your own backyard, then in an afternoon, you can have your wish. Now water garden creation is easier than ever, because you can purchase everything you need either in kit form or as individual components. The basics are easy. You need a structure, waterproof liner, and pump system to circulate the water. You can add sound-enhancing options, such as waterfalls or fountains. Essential parts of a water garden ecosystem are plants and fish. Floating plants such as water lettuce or water hyacinth help shade the fish (koi or goldfish), whose job is to keep the water garden free of mosquito larvae. Even the smallest water gardens are teeming with life.

1 BUILD THE WALLS. Determine the location of the water garden. Placing it near a window in your house allows you to enjoy the sound of water both inside and out. The ground must be solid and level. Stack the bricks into a rectangular shape.

2 INSERT THE PADDING. The precut padding is positioned on the bottom of the water garden to protect the plastic liner.

3 COVER WITH THE LINER. Drape the liner inside the water garden structure. Allow an ample amount of liner to overlap on all sides.

4 FILL WITH WATER. With the liner firmly in place, fill the structure with water. The weight of the water will settle the liner into the bottom of the structure.

5 CUT THE LINER TO FIT. Cut the excess liner away, making sure the edges line up with the outer edges of the top stones. Place the top layer of stones on top of the cut liner.

6 POSITION THE WATERFALL. Place the waterfall from the kit in the water, setting it at the back edge of the water garden structure.

7 CONNECT THE PUMP. Using the kit instructions, connect the pump to the waterfall.

8 PLACE ROCKS AND STONE. To hide the waterfall and pump features, place decorative stones on top. Adjust the look of the waterfall by adding and taking away stones. As a final detail, you can add river-smoothed stones and votive candles to the scene.

GETTING THE LOOK

MATERIALS

- Pallet of tumbled blocks
- Water garden kit that includes padding, liner, waterfall, pump, and lights
- Decorative stones
- 3 goldfish
- Potted papyrus
- 3 water lettuce plants

Adding submerged lighting to a water-garden feature creates lovely, luminous light—and extends the use of a patio area long after sunset. A timer kit allows you to set the time that the lights turn on and off.

Lights, Please!

A B
C D

1712
SIXTIETH STREET

Lighting has its theatrical side, but there's more to it than fancy footlights and floodlights. Lighting also provides an element of safety and security to your home and landscape.

With the flick of a switch or the strike of a match, you can instantly shed new light on your yard and garden after the sun has gone down. You can create lighted accents throughout your yard that highlight your home, provide stepping safety in the dark, and create evening ambience that is simply magical. Whether you choose to go high-tech with inground low-voltage electrical lighting, harness the power of the sun with solar lights, or go the old-fashioned route with candlelight, there are many easy-to-install lighting options that will allow you to spend more time enjoying your yard and garden after dark.

Traditional electric lighting offers a range of low-voltage options that can alter your yard's look.

PATH LIGHTING

Although lighting along pathways is decorative, it also illuminates the pathway so walkers can make their way from point A to point B in the dark. Place pathway lighting 1 to 2 feet off the ground to cast light directly on the path. Avoid eye-level lighting, which can take the eye's focus away from where you or your guests need to go.

UPLIGHTING

The most theatrical lighting option, uplighting allows you to throw light upward onto an object. Spotlights can train a narrow beam into a tree or onto a piece of statuary or art in order to highlight it in a darkened landscape.

FLOODLIGHTS

Floodlights provide a broader wash of light and are used to highlight larger areas such as the front entryway of a home or specific architectural elements such as a wide front porch.

SOLAR OPTIONS

Solar lights offer the ultimate in convenience and cost. Install them (usually without tools), and the sun's rays do the rest. Solar lighting is perfect for ambience lighting of pathways, flower beds, and borders. But new models featuring brighter light-emitting diodes (LEDs) allow solar lighting to compete with low-voltage alternatives.

LIGHT THE NIGHT

A STRIP LIGHTING
Typically used during the holiday season, strip lighting creates an easy alternative to more complex lighting options. Strip lighting lies directly on the ground and provides a surprising amount of upward illumination. Strands can be connected so you can use this lighting effect for long borders.

B CANDLELIGHT
The simplest of all lighting options (just strike a match), candlelight is also the most romantic. Candles are the perfect ambience-creating light sources. From sparkling votives to large candles positioned directly on the ground, the soft glowing light from candles is rivaled only by starlight. Candles are portable. They should be used only in places where there is no chance they could be overturned.

C TABLETOP LIGHTING
Strands of twinkle lights rolled into a ball are capped by green glass garden cloches to make this unusual (but garden-appropriate) tabletop lighting feature.

D SOLAR LIGHTING
Solar lighting is more popular than ever, with many options for homeowners to use. Easy to install, solar lights are stuck directly into the ground without wires or connectors. Solar lighting options include inset ground lighting, spots, and aboveground pathway lighting.

Lights, Please!
Wake Up the night

Lighting your garden and landscape has never been easier. There are many low-cost options that you can install yourself with a minimum of time and tools.

TIME NEEDED
2 to 4
HOURS

You can create drama with the flick of a switch (or the setting of a timer). Lighting up your landscape after the sun has gone down extends after-hours activity in your yard and garden.

A dark landscape is at best uninviting, and at worst, dangerous. Simple, easy-to-install lighting options allow you to place lights where they enhance the beauty of your home's exterior, landscaping features, and plantings—offering a safer way for you and your guests to enjoy your home after the sun has gone down. In addition to ambience, outdoor lighting also produces an element of safety. Intruders may be deterred by well-lit doorways and windows.

BEFORE

AFTER!
A combination of lighting options makes this house more accessible— and safer—on dark nights.

You can skip calling an electrician to light up your landscape. Low-voltage systems are easy to install, safe, and economical. By using low-voltage options, you can do it all yourself—in just a few hours.

Inexpensive holiday lighting (also called strip or tube lighting) can be used in beds and borders to create a magical uplighting effect. With edging plants softly growing above them in the summer and a white snow cover in the winter, these lights will offer a muted glow all year long. And when they burn out, you can easily and quickly replace them for about $10 to $12 per strand.

Simple strip lighting on the ground makes a luminous glow and uplighting effect.

 **1**

 **2**

 **3**

 **4**

 **5**

BECOME THE NIGHTTIME STAR OF THE NEIGHBORHOOD

1 PLUG IT IN. Before you start this lighting project, plug in the lighting strip to make sure it works. Then roll it out and position it on the ground.

2 ATTACH BRACKETS. On the back of a garden edging strip, screw in a bracket to hold the strip in place (most lighting strips come with this hardware).

3 POSITION LIGHTING STRIPS. Snap the lighting strip into the bracket on the back of the edging.

4 LIGHT UP THE STONES. To add strip lighting to stone edgers, position the strip on the ground and hold in place by inserting U-pins over the strip.

5 TIME IT. To automate your lighting, plug the strip connector into an outdoor light timer. For safety, schedule the lights to go on at dusk and off at dawn.

EXPERT TIP The type of lighting (and where you place it in the landscape) should depend on how you use the spaces in your yard. Consider a combination of lighting options for a unified effect. For example, use path lighting in conjunction with silhouetting or uplighting to make a dark landscape come alive at night.

Case Study
Sensational Spa Area

AFTER!

Scented plants, flowering vines, soft towels, and a table-top water garden make an inviting outdoor spa experience.

PART
#1

PART
#2

PART
#3

GETTING THE LOOK

SHOPPING LIST

THE SPA AREA
- Bistro table
- 2 bistro chairs
- 2 large ceramic planters
- Flat-backed door planter
- 3 trellises
- 9 screw-in hooks
- 3 towels

THE PLANTS
- 2 Madagascar jasmine vines
- 1 potted Mandevilla vine
- 2 black-eyed Susan vines
- 'Endless Summer' hydrangea
- Yellow lantana

THE TABLETOP WATER GARDEN
- Ceramic bowl
- Small, smooth stones
- 6 water lettuce plants

BEFORE

Oregano

Lavender

Mint

Scented Geranium

Madagascar Jasmine

Lilac

Part One: Setting the Scene

How do you turn a hot-tub area into a spa-worthy space? Here's the basic math: paint plus plantings plus props equals pizzazz.

TIME NEEDED
2 to 4 HOURS

Everyone in the family wanted a hot tub, but now that it's installed on the concrete slab beside the garage, it looks unappealing. That's the dilemma many homeowners face when they buy an aboveground hot tub. But there are secrets to decorating around a large, square object the size of a small car and tying its luxury use into an equally luxurious landscape.

SURVEYING THE SITE

Situated on the west side of the garage, this open spa area is perfect for sunset viewing and late-night stargazing. The concrete base (with drain) is required to level the hot tub, but the area around the tub also serves as a small, intimate patio area. Dressed up with a fresh coat of paint on the walls and floor, small-space furniture, and fantastically fragrant plants, the hot-tub area is transformed from barren to bountiful.

CREATING A SPA ENVIRONMENT

In addition to the soothing bubbling waters that a hot tub offers, a true spa experience requires stimulation of more senses. Scent, color, and comfort are all supporting roles in the overall relaxation experience.

SWEETENING IT UP

Infusing fragrance into a spa area is easy when you plant sweet-smelling flower varieties. Madagascar jasmine (*Stephanotis floribunda*) produces lovely white, fleshy flowers that perfume the area with their sweet scent. These climbing vines can be planted in decorative pots, then trained onto wall-hung trellises to create a garden of scented delight.

SCENTED CONTAINER PLANTINGS

For a spa area or backyard patio where the plants are viewed at close range, get double duty from them by planting gorgeous varieties that also smell sweet. Here are some options:

MADAGASCAR JASMINE (*STEPHANOTIS FLORIBUNDA*)

JAPANESE TREE LILAC (*SYRINGA RETICULATA*)

ROSE (*ROSA*)

SCENTED GERANIUM (*PELARGONIUM*)

FLOWERING TOBACCO (*NICOTIANA*)

LAVENDER (*LAVANDULA*)

THYME (*THYMUS*)

OREGANO (*ORIGANUM*)

LEMON VERBENA (*ALOYSIA TRIPHYLLA*)

MINT (*MENTHA*)

Case Study
Sensational Spa Area

PART
#2

Part Two:
Terrific Trellis

Painted garden trellises double as plant supports and a towel rack.

TIME NEEDED
30 to 60 MINS.

CREATING CREATURE COMFORTS

A bistro table and chairs allow visitors to enjoy the spa area when not steeping in the hot tub. A towel rack hung with plush terry cloth towels is made from a trellis, painted blue, turned upside down, and hung on the very hooks that support the towels. Two matching trellises serve their original purpose as supports for plants—the two fragrant Madagascar jasmines. The color scheme, influenced by water, sun, and sky, features plant selections in blue and white with accents of pink and yellow. Earth-inspired hues are soothing and relaxing—the perfect color scheme for a backyard spa retreat.

1

2

3

1 HOOK IT. Screw in three hooks at the appropriate level for the height of the trellis. Hang the trellis.

2 VINE IT. Use twine to tie vines of climbing plants (planted into containers) onto the trellis.

3 HANG IT. Use one trellis as a towel rack.

1

2

3

4

Part Three:
Bowl Full of Beauty

TIME NEEDED
15 to 30
MINS.

A tabletop water garden is easy to make when you use floating plants such as water lettuce.

1 ADD SMOOTH STONES. Start with a ceramic bowl about 6 inches deep. Add a few smooth stones to the bottom of the bowl.

2 FILL THE BOWL WITH WATER. Pour fresh lukewarm water into the bowl. Fill to the brim.

3 SEPARATE WATER LETTUCE. Water lettuce has a dense root system. Separate the plants from one another and place them upright on the surface of the water.

4 MONITOR THE WATER LEVEL. Keep the garden's water level at the top of the bowl's lip. Treat this water garden as a temporary arrangement—like cut flowers—and discard the water lettuce when it starts to fade. NOTE: Keep water lettuce away from open waterways. It is invasive in some climates.

CHAPTER FOUR

SPEEDING UP THE LONG TERM

The evolution of a landscape and garden is an ongoing event. Every plant has an established growth rate, but there are tricks to speeding up the long-term possibilities of a landscape's great looks.

In this chapter...

Pumping Up Your Plants

Plants have simple needs. Some great soil. Water when they need it. Sunshine or shade, depending on their variety. A nutritious snack once in a while. And some physical therapy—pruning or dividing—once in a greater while.

The key to pumped-up plants is providing them with the right stuff. The plants in your garden are engineered to look their best when they are growing in the right environment—with the correct nutrients. They'll do fine in a wide range of growing situations—but for maximum impact, you'll want to make growing conditions as optimal as possible.

The Dirt on Soil

Starting with good soil is important. In order for plants to really set down their roots, they need rich loamy soil that nourishes and supports them. Since you rarely get to choose what sort of soil your house is built on (and in many cases, the topsoil has been removed during building so the soil left behind is clay, sand, or rocks—something less than perfect for plant growth), you will need to amend your soil to make it more robust and healthy. In some cases, you can bring in new soil.

LOAM
Loam—40 percent sand, 20 percent clay, 40 percent silt—is the soil most coveted by gardeners. It's dark and richly colored, with an earthy aroma. Its composition and texture are a balance of sand, silt, clay, and organic material. This combination is ideal because it allows water, air, and nutrients to flow downward to the roots of the plant. The lightweight, noncompacted texture also means loam is home to worms and other soil-benefitting organisms. The texture of loam snugly anchors roots, yet permits them to spread. Loamy soil is easy to dig in too.

SAND
Sandy soils features larger rock particles separated by wide-open air pockets. The spaces between the particles allow water to drain too fast, often carrying nutrients away from plant roots. Because there is little organic material in sandy soils, they dry out quickly, even after substantial rainfall. They heat up fast during the day, then cool down equally quickly when the sun goes down. The continual soil-temperature changes put unhealthy stress on plants. Sand is an essential component of loamy soil because it loosens clay and silt particles; sand should make up roughly 40 percent of a soil's content.

HOW TO TREAT To remedy sandy soil, mix in composted organic matter or ready-to-use packaged garden soil to bind the soil particles, improve water retention, stabilize roots, augment nutrients, and establish a loamy consistency attractive to earthworms and other helpful organisms. Work in perlite to plug air pockets.

Clay Soil

Loam

Soil sediment test

CLAY

Clay is the opposite end of the soil spectrum from sand. Clay soil is compacted and has few air pockets. Its particles are fine, flat, and packed tightly together. The result is a plant-resistant soil that stunts root growth and is nearly impossible to till or dig because of its weight and density. When it rains, clay accumulates water, and puddles may form on top. Consequently, clay encourages root rot in plants. Although clay is rich in minerals, its mass discourages soil-friendly organisms from working the soil.

HOW TO TREAT: Thin clay by adding ready-to-use packaged garden soil, composted organic matter and soil conditioners to break up clay particles. Avoid sandbox sand, which can turn clay soil into concretelike chunks.

Watering

Simply stated, water is life. A plant's need for water varies, depending on the species. Obviously, plants from desert or arid regions do fine with less water than, say, tropicals that are used to a daily shower on their home turf. Here are some basic watering rules:

WATER OFTEN IN THE SUMMER. Most plants need more water in the summer because of evaporation and drying winds.

WATER WHEN TEMPERATURES ARE COOLEST. Water evaporates less overnight. If fungus is a problem, you should water first thing in the morning.

WATER DEEPLY. Frequent, shallow watering encourages shallow roots that react adversely under drought or hot conditions.

AVOID OVERDOING IT. Water is good, but too much can hurt your plants. Water only as much as the soil can absorb. Make sure all containers have adequate drainage.

CONSIDER DRIP IRRIGATION. Drip irrigation systems allow water to enter the soil slowly, penetrating the root zone with minimum surface wetting.

MULCH IT. Mulch conserves soil moisture, reduces water run-off, allows better water penetration into the root mass, and limits weed growth.

AMENDMENTS FOR SICKLY SOIL

You can remedy any type of soil with the right amendments:

SHREDDED NEWSPAPER is a good addition to clay or sandy soil. Make sure it is well shredded; then lay it on top of a bed and cover it with grass clippings.

COCOA SHELLS are byproducts of chocolate manufacturing. The shells break down into nutrients when used as mulch for both sandy and clay soils.

SAWDUST provides woody fiber to clay soil by breaking down the tightly packed clay particles. Spread as a 2-inch layer of mulch.

STRAW is great for improving the aeration and drainage of clay-heavy soils. Spread as a 2-inch mulch, straw is ideal for vegetable gardens.

GYPSUM is a mineral composed of calcium sulfate. Mix pelletized gypsum into the top 2 inches of soil to provide aeration in clay.

PEAT MOSS is harvested from bogs and is ideal as an organic amendment for both sandy and clay soils. Mix 2 inches of peat moss into the top 6 inches of soil.

Soil amendments above include sulfur (to decrease pH), compost, lime (to raise pH), and peat (to lower pH).

Pumping Up Your Plants
Feeding

Feeding

Your garden needs to eat. The types of plant food that you serve (as well as the ingredients and frequency) depend on what plants are growing in your garden.

NUTRIENT COMPOSITION

There are three essential nutrients in plant food, and each serves a specific purpose in making a great-looking, healthy plant. Nitrogen (N) promotes the growth of leaves and stems. To getter bigger, greener, more robust plants, you need nitrogen. Phosphorus (P) and potassium (K) increase flowering and root growth.

THE NUTRIENT MIX

Plant foods are labeled according to the percentages of the three nutrients they contain. Labels always list percentage components in this order: nitrogen, phosphorus, potassium (N-P-K). That means that a plant food label that is marked 15-30-15 has equal parts nitrogen and potassium and twice that amount of phosphorus. Different plants have different feeding needs. However, a slow-release plant food that contains a fairly equal amount of nitrogen, phosphorous, and potassium will cover the feeding needs of nearly everything in a landscape.

10-10-10 Guaranteed Analysis	F1198	
Total Nitrogen (N)*..10%		Derived from Polymer-coated, S
10.0% Ammoniacal Nitrogen		Ammonium Phosphate and Pota
Available Phosphate (P$_2$O$_5$)*..............................10%		*The Nitrogen, Phosphate and P
Soluble Potash (K$_2$O)*..10%		coated to provide 7.0% slow rel
Sulfur (S) (Total)..20%		release Phosphate (P$_2$O$_5$) and 7
4.0% Combined Sulfur (S)		Information regarding the conten
16.0% Free Sulfur (S)		is available on the internet at ht

CHOOSING THE RIGHT TYPE

There are plant foods made for different types of gardens and gardeners. Here is the rundown.

WATER SOLUBLE

Water soluble plant food is mixed with water and distributed to garden plants through a hose and feeder combination or watering can. This type of plant food is most often used by professional growers because it's easy to apply and to control the amount of nutrients being delivered. The results of water-soluble plant food are apparent in a few days. These products are great for larger flowers and vegetables, and you can repeat applications every other week or so to get healthier plants and larger flowers.

Deadhead to Bolster Bloom

Removing the spent blossoms from both annuals and perennial plants helps the plant produce more flowers. When you remove the dead blooms from annual plants, you "trick" the plant into producing more flowers. When a plant produces a flower, it does so to create seed to reproduce itself. Removing the flower triggers the plant to produce more flowers. Annuals that will produce more blooms with deadheading include pansies and zinnas. Some annual plants don't need deadheading, such as impatiens and some self-cleaning petunia varieties. For perennials, deadheading may not produce additional blooms, but it does neaten the appearance of the plant. For some perennials (and roses), the dried seed heads (and hips) are a food source for birds, as well as an attractive aspect of the plant that can be enjoyed during the winter. Also, if you want to collect seeds from perennials, you must allow the seed heads to mature.

CONTINUOUS RELEASE

This easy-to-use plant food type allows you to apply nutrients to plants as you plant them. You can spread it around plants on top of the soil or mix it in with the soil when you plant. You can also apply it directly into planting holes before you plant. Slow release plant food feeds plants steadily and consistently for several months. Most granular plant foods contain a mix of nutrients that are immediately available to the plants after watering or rainfall. Overall, they are an economical plant food that can be purchased in formulations created for specific types of plants.

GOING ORGANIC

For gardeners choosing to garden naturally, there are organic plant food options. Miracle-Gro Organic Choice garden plant food contains 100 percent organic ingredients including pelletized chicken manure.

Divide to Keep Healthy

Because perennials grow bigger each year, they may have to be divided at some point. The good news is that most perennial plants can be divided easily. Dividing plants is more than a great way to renew an old or overgrown plant—it is also an inexpensive way to get more plants for elsewhere in the garden or to help build and diversify the gardens of your friends. The easiest perennials to divide are those that grow in clumps, such as catmint, daylilies, and spiderwort.

The best time to divide is early spring, when the new growth is just beginning to emerge. You can either dig the entire clump up and break it into pieces, or you can split the plant in two, leaving half in the ground and removing the other half.

Although most perennials respond well to division, some are less amenable. These include baptisia, gas plant, baby's breath, Oriental poppies, and hollyhocks. Plants with woody roots such as goatsbeard are also best left undivided.

Bigger Can Be Better

When you plant the biggest trees, shrubs, or perennials you can find (and afford), you attain instant results—and a landscape that looks like it's been there for a long time.

Conventional wisdom says "bigger is better," and that is certainly true when it comes to instant gardens. When you purchase and plant larger plants, you can speed up the finished look of your garden by years.

INSTANT IMPACT TREES

Trees are the most costly plant you can buy for your landscape—especially if you purchase large ones. Trees grow slowly. A small, inexpensive bare-root sapling (which could be mistaken for a stick) may already be several years old and still look a little lost when planted in a yard—certainly it will be years before it is large enough to cast some shade or handle a tire swing.

So for those who want instant impact—and can afford the sticker price—a large tree is the way to go. A more mature tree planted in a new landscape will look as if it has been growing there for years.

Large trees—those with trunks that measure 2 inches or more in diameter—can be either grown in containers or harvested from the ground. Field- or nursery-grown trees have substantially larger root balls than those grown in containers and are heavier and more difficult to move and plant. Moving and transplanting a large tree with a tree spade requires professional expertise, not only in the unearthing and transportation, but also in the planting techniques required for specific species. Planting a large tree should be left in the capable hands (and tree spade) of an experienced tree care professional.

SPECIALTY TREES

Some landscapers specialize in native and regionally specific trees. For example, you can buy mature live oaks in Texas, full-size palms in Florida, and giant saguaro cacti in Arizona. When ordering native or specialty species, you should work with a reputable landscaper who is knowledgeable about the growth requirements of specific trees.

SUPER-SIZED SHRUBS

You get more bang for your landscape buck when you buy large shrubs. You can purchase shrubs in three sizes (from the largest to the smallest: balled-and-burlapped, container, and bare-root), although many large shrubs are sold only in containers.

Planting larger shrubs is a winning proposition because they often cost little more than smaller versions. And even the largest shrubs (such as 10-foot-tall arborvitae) can be planted by one person (although two people make it easier).

PUMPED-UP PERENNIALS

Perennials can be purchased either in containers or bare root. Big perennials, sold in 5-gallon pots, create instant impact in a garden when planted in a bed or border. Great for creating a new bed that looks established or replacing a perennial that has died in an existing border, large-scale perennials adapt well to transplanting. Be vigilant about water and mulch to make sure that the adjustment from pot to ground is as easy as possible.

You can buy the same varieties in several forms. For example, you can buy the same rose as bare-root stock (usually the mail-order option); container grown, in full bloom; or container grown, in dormancy.

THE TRADEOFFS OF SUPER-SIZING YOUR LANDSCAPE

The tradeoffs to buying bigger plants—trees, shrubs, and perennials—for your landscape boil down to two words: time and money. If you have more money than time, go big. But if you decide to plant smaller-stature choices, especially shrubs and perennials, your purchases will catch up to their larger cousins in a matter of years. When you purchase large-scale plants, buy stock from reliable nurseries that can give you advice about the planting and care of your purchase. Since large plants are inherently more costly than small ones, getting a plant guarantee is important.

A Japanese maple in three forms: bare-root, young sapling, and several-year-old tree. The major differences are plant age and, consequently, plant price.

TRANSPLANTING A LARGE TREE

MOVING LARGE TREES IS BIG BUSINESS. LANDSCAPERS USE TREE MOVERS, CALLED TREE SPADES, THAT CAN TRANSPLANT 15-FOOT-TALL EVERGREENS OR DECIDUOUS TREES WITH A TRUNK DIAMETER OF 6 TO 8 INCHES. HERE ARE SOME THINGS TO THINK ABOUT BEFORE GOING WITH THE BIGGER-IS-BETTER-ROUTE IN TREES:

• Before you plant, make sure your landscaper has approved the new location in respect to climate zone, wind exposure, soil moisture and drainage, and compatibility with the existing vegetation.

• The bigger the tree, the longer its recovery after transplanting. The general rule is that the tree takes one year for every inch of tree diameter to recover. That means that a 6-inch tree could take six years to resume growth.

• When buying a large tree, make sure to get a guarantee. Most reputable landscapers offer a warranty on large trees.

• To ensure transition of a new tree transplant, make sure the soil is right for the tree and that it is properly fed after planting.

• Stake newly transplanted extra-large trees because they are bound to be top heavy and could topple in a strong wind. Allow a bit of give to the staking wires and remove after about two years.

• After a large deciduous tree is transplanted, prune about one third of the tree's branches to help create a balance between the branches and the roots. Remove small interior branches, keeping the height and width of the tree the same.

1 THE FORKS of the tree spade are inserted around the tree, and the tree is pulled from the ground.

2 HAVING BEEN soaked overnight, the earth remains intact around the roots of the tree until planting.

3 THE TREE travels by truck to its destined location.

THE BEST BIG TREES FOR TRANSPLANTING
Depending on your area, there are some trees that will transplant better than others. To research the guidelines for tree transplanting by species, refer to the "American Standard for Nursery Stock," published by the American Nursery & Landscape Association online at www.anla.org.

Annuals

Annual flowers come in a paint-box assortment of bloom colors and foliage possibilities.

Perennials

Perennials return year after year, and each variety has its own particular bloom season.

STYLE CONSIDERATIONS No matter what style your garden or yard is, there are annuals that fit the bill. They bloom in nearly every color, and they grow from short to tall. Popular annuals include geranium, petunia, celosia, salvia, zinnia, marigold, and sweet alyssum. Because of their adaptable nature and all-season bloom, annuals are ideal for window boxes and containers. The come in many forms that allow them to fit into any garden scheme: vining, trailing, mounding, and upright.

DURABILITY Just as their name suggests, annuals last for only one season. Whether you grow them in your garden from seed or buy already started plants, they are growing with a mission—to flower and set seed. Deadheading their faded blooms helps prolong their cycle—and keeps them producing new flowers. But in the end, most annuals will die when the first frost blackens their foliage.

COST FACTORS You can buy small annuals in 6- or 8-packs for very little cost, but they take longer to mature. Annuals are also sold in 4-inch pots—and even in gallon containers. Generally, the larger the annual, the more it will cost.

STYLE CONSIDERATIONS Perennials are a huge class of plants, so you have a wide range of possibilities when using them in the garden. They come in sizes from short to tall and offer fabulous flower types—trumpet-shaped blooms, wide-petaled beauties, flower spikes, balls of bloom, and some that are beyond description in their intricacies.

DURABILITY Perennials return each year, getting bigger and better as time passes. The caveat to this is that they must be planted in the right zone, in the right soil, and in the right light to prosper.

COST FACTORS Perennials cost more than annuals and are worth it in that they are a permanent planting. As you might expect, rare perennials (those not grown in mass production) may be costly. Perennial aficionados are often willing to pay the price.

OTHER TYPES OF PLANTS

BULBS A huge plant class of their own, bulbs offer flowers in spring, summer, and fall. Spring-blooming bulbs include tulip, hyacinth, narcissus, squill, and crocus. Spring-blooming bulbs are perennial, and some spread, getting bigger and denser every year. Summer-blooming bulbs, such as calla, dahlia, and caladium, are tender and must be lifted from the ground and stored indoors for the winter. Lilies are summer-blooming bulbs that can be left in the garden.

Shrubs

Ornamental shrubs add color and form to any landscape.

Trees

Trees are the slowest growing of the plant groups, but are the longest lived.

STYLE CONSIDERATIONS Shrubs offer landscapers a wide selection of plant colors, forms, and heights. For every landscape purpose, there is a shrub. Low-growing and spreading shrubs, such as creeping juniper, are perfect solutions for foundation coverups. Blooming shrubs, such as forsythia, lilac, and azalea, offer a spring flower show. Evergreen shrubs, such as yew, boxwood, and holly, provide privacy, living fences, and all-season interest.

DURABILITY In general, shrubs are durable. If planted in the correct zone and light placement, they will grow and flourish for decades.

COST FACTORS Buying small shrubs is the best value. But these tiny plants are for gardeners with patience. If you want an established look to your landscape, buying big is the way to go.

STYLE CONSIDERATIONS Good-looking, healthy trees add value to a home. Trees soften and shade the landscape and even help cut down on utility usage. Trees come in a wide range of styles and growth habits. And they come in varied leaf types—the most general being deciduous (those that drop their leaves every year and grow new ones) and coniferous (those that retain their leaves year round).

DURABILITY Slow-growing trees are extremely durable. Fast-growing trees, such as willow and poplar, are useful if you need quick cover, but they are usually short-lived and have weak wood, causing branches to break. Hardwoods, such as oaks and maples, are slower growing but will last for centuries.

COST FACTORS Tree prices depend on their size—from bare-root saplings to 30-foot giants you move with a tree spade.

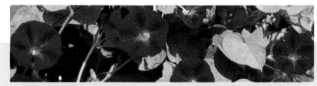

VINES Vines like to stretch out and travel. Available as both annuals and perennials, vines include those grown for showy flowers (wisteria, honeysuckle, trumpet, morning glory) and attractive foliage (ivy, Virginia creeper). They are excellent choices to train onto fences, arbors, and arches.

TROPICALS A wide range of plants are called tropicals because they are from areas of the world that are hotter and more temperate than most areas of the United States. Using these plants in gardens is a fun way to introduce an exotic element. Tropicals include any plant that cannot withstand frost, such as banana, citrus trees, and palms. Many plants grown as annuals are actually tropical perennials

CACTI Cacti are a massive plant class, offering varieties that are covered with spines and other protective outerwear. Although many are from desert climates, some are hardy in colder climates.

Layering for Mass Effect

Layering is a planting method that increases the plant density of a space by combining trees, shrubs, and plants in a tiered placement. By filling both horizontal and vertical space, you create a sense of lushness and maturity right away.

Mounds of lush Japanese fountain grass create an undulating effect in this border.

In the plant world, growth equals time. To speed up the clock in your own yard, plant in layers. Nothing makes a landscape look more lush and filled-in than plants in a stacked formation. After all, that's how nature does it. By layering levels of groundcovers, flowers and foliage, shrubs, and trees, you are replicating the methods of nature. Look at any naturally established area, and you'll find a stair-stepped growth pattern—from forests to deserts. Those landscapes, of course, were created over millions of years. What can you do in a weekend?

A LESSON FROM THE WOODS

If you take a walk in the woods, you'll see that nature fills in the space in an attractive and efficient way. Small lichens and mosses grow amid and on top of rocks. Larger-leaved groundcovers, such as ivies, small ferns, and Jack-in-the-pulpits, fill in the gaps on the woodland floor. Above them the space is filled with taller-stemmed foliar plants. The next horizontal level is the understory—small trees and shrubs that grow in the soft shade provided by the canopy. The large old-growth trees of the forest create the leafy canopy.

EXPERT TIP **MADE IN THE SHADE**
As a layered garden matures, it becomes a shade garden. But keep in mind that even in the darkest shade, bright flowers can bloom. Colorful flowers for shady spots include columbine, woodland phlox, violet, bleeding heart, anemone, bluebell, at right, and goatsbeard.

RIGHT Creating a lovely layered look works best when you choose plants from all groups—trees or shrubs, understory trees, tall perennials, and edging plants. Here, Japanese maple casts shade over a garden of hosta and sedum. FAR RIGHT Yellow flag iris and lady's mantle snuggle under the boughs of a Japanese maple to anchor the edge of a pond. BELOW A river birch grows in the shade of a pine tree.

NATURE'S LOGIC

You can use the same logic of this stair-step growing plan in your own garden by purchasing plants that will grow together in a stacked group. By planning and planting in this way, you are creating new growing opportunities in your yard. For example, when you plant a large tree, you are also creating an area of shade that was not previously there. Planting in layers creates a symbiotic relationship that also effectively and naturally fills in space—both horizontally and vertically.

LAYERING A GARDEN

To get an instant impact layered look, plant in height levels so that wherever you plant—a bed, border, island bed, or foundation area—you've also created a stacked effect of plantings. By looking at your planting area as both vertical and horizontal space, you can start filling in the blanks.

BOTTOMS UP

If you look at your yard as a box of space, you can better understand how you can fill that space. Start with the bottom. The ground level contains areas for low-growing plants that cover the earth. If your top layer provides adequate shade, you can plant low-light tolerant perennials such as hosta, vinca, or small varieties of ferns. If your top layer initially is too immature to provide the shade needed for most shade plants, choose a groundcover that will tolerate both shade and partial shade locations.

BETWEEN THE GROUND AND THE SKY

Midrange space can be filled with perennial plants that grow 1 to 2 feet high, small shrubs such as Japanese barberry or rockspray cotoneaster, and understory trees such as Japanese maple, serviceberry, or hawthorn. The plants in the understory of a forest must be able to tolerate partial shade and be shorter at maturity than the overstory trees. Many ornamental trees, such as dogwoods and redbuds, are perfect understory trees because they grow best in the dappled shade provided by taller trees.

ADDING HEIGHT

The overstory, or canopy, is the layer of tallest trees. Height can be relative, however, when it comes to landscaping your yard. There are a great number of shade trees that can be planted as the top level. Good shade tree species include red maple, sugar maple, horsechestnut, sycamore, and oaks (white, red, burr, and pin).

THE STORY ON UNDERSTORY TREES

Many smaller trees grow well in the dappled shade provided by large shade trees or, in urban spaces, by buildings. These small trees are ideal choices for home gardens because they are more in scale with smaller yards where space and light may be at a premium.

AMERICAN HORNBEAM, IRONWOOD
(OSTRYA VIRGINIANA)

CAROLINA SILVERBELL
(HALESIA CAROLINA)

FLOWERING DOGWOOD
(CORNUS FLORIDA)

KOUSA DOGWOOD
(CORNUS KOUSA)

PAGODA DOGWOOD
(CORNUS ALTERNIFOLIA)

SERVICEBERRY
(AMELANCHIER CANADENSIS)

EASTERN REDBUD
(CERCIS CANADENSIS)

CHAPTER FOUR
**Speeding Up
the Long Term**

Large Leaves

A B
C D

Sweet potato vine produces large, heart-shaped leaves in chocolate brown, lime green, and green and yellow bicolors.

Large-leaved plants quickly infuse your garden with a feeling of exotic luxury and tropicalismo.

If small, delicate plants are the whisperers in your garden, then large-leaved foliage plants are the Ethel Mermans. No shy retiring types, these. Foliage plants with large leaves can add instant impact to your garden by infusing it with exotic leaf textures, colors, and styles. Plus, large-leafed plants can create a lush look with less plants.

TROPICAL EXOTICS
When you want to really leaf out your landscape, add tropical plants. Even gardeners in northern climates can enjoy the exotic foliage of large-leaved tropical plants during the summer. In fact, the hot, humid summer weather of many northern gardens is the perfect growing environment for these equatorial beauties.

There are many varieties of palms with attractive foliage fans. Palms grow quickly and can reach great heights even as potted plants. But the best thing about palms is that they are inexpensive—you can frequently purchase large plants for as little as $10, so you can guiltlessly treat them as annuals.

GO BANANAS
Bananas (*Musaceae*) grow in Zones 8 to 11 in the United States but can be purchased as potted plants in cooler zones during the summer. They grow 5 to 8 feet tall and are topped with lush large leaves. Some banana varieties have solid green leaves. Red-leaved banana (*Ensete ventricosum* 'Maurelii') offers red-tinged leaves that are

as colorful as any flower. Pineapples are members of the bromeliad family, which offers large and exotic foliage as well as beautiful flowers. Canna, grown from tender rhizomes, come in a kaleidoscope of colors and stripes. 'Tropicana' produces striped multicolored leaves topped with radiant orange flowers. Ginger lilies (*Hedychium* spp.) are subtropical plants hardy in Zones 8–11. They can be grown in cooler climates, producing rhizomes that can be lifted and overwintered in the same way that cannas are. Elephant's ear (*Colocasia esculenta*) grow from tubers; plants reach 10 feet or more. The giant leaves measure 1 foot or more across.

LARGE AND LUXURIOUS
In shady areas, a wide variety of large-leaved hostas will spread their umbrella crowns to cover 3 to 4 feet of ground beneath them. 'Sagae' bears 13- to 14-inch leaves. Also for shady spots, ferns offer large lacy leaves that can transform a woodland floor into a soft, verdant carpet. Marginal wood fern (*Dryopteris marginalis*) has thick coppery leafstalks that grow 1 to 2 feet long. Wood fern (*Dryopteris intermedia*) produces graceful, arching fronds that grow 2 feet tall. Ostrich fern (*Matteuccia struthiopteris*) and royal fern (*Osmunda regalis*) both offer extravagant 6-foot-tall fronds. Castor bean (*Ricinus communis*) is also a stellar grower, producing large-stemmed, textured leaves that are lobed like fingers.

LARGE AND LOVELY

A GUNNERA (*GUNNERA MANICATA*)
This overachieving plant produces leaves than can measure several feet across. Plant gunnera in a moist spot where it can strut its stuff.

B ELEPHANT'S EAR (*COLOCASIA ESCULENTA*)
Also called taro, this tender perennial produces large, heart-shaped leaves that measure up to 3 feet across.

C CANNA 'TROPICANA' (*CANNA ×GENERALIS*)
This showy canna's leaves outshine its flowers. The yellow-and-green-striped leaves are almond-shaped and measure several feet long.

D PERSIAN SHIELD (*STROBILANTHES DYERIANUS*)
The colorful seersucker leaves of Persian shield measure up to 7 inches long.

OTHER LARGE-LEAVED PLANTS

RUBBER TREE (*FICUS ELASTICA*)

SPLIT-LEAF PHILODENDRON (*MONSTERA DELICIOSA*)

DRACAENA (*DRACAENA FRAGRANS*)

SWEET POTATO VINE (*IPOMOEA BATATAS*)

LILY-OF-THE-NILE (*AGAPHANTHUS AFRICANUS*)

COLEUS (*SOLENOSTEMON SCUTELLARIOIDES*)

Long-Season Color
Flowers and Foliage

Select from hundreds of plants—annuals, perennials, shrubs, and trees—to paint your garden with color all season.

There are certain plant species that never seem to have bad days. In other words, no matter what the weather or season, they just look great. Maybe it's their long-season bloom, maybe it's their fantastic foliage, or maybe it's their shape or form. For instant impact all season, try these naturals in your garden.

EVER-BLOOMING ANNUALS

Annuals are the go-getters of the garden. For long-season color, nothing beats their consistent blooms. Revel in the sunny yellows of marigold and sunflower. The citrusy hot oranges of Mexican sunflower and zinnia. The sizzling reds of geranium and celosia. The bright blues of salvia and lobelia. Annuals offer long-season color in any palette you need—from blazing hot to soft pastels. Once they start blooming in spring, they keep it up until frost. These flower factories are the perfect plants to use if you like to change the color scheme of your garden from year to year.

PERSISTENT PERENNIALS

By nature, perennials bloom just once a year, but they return year after year for the same command performance. And although each perennial has a finite bloom period, there are some species that flower longer than others. Some perennials are such overachievers that they will bloom twice in one season if sheared back after the first flush of bloom. In addition, there are a number of perennials that feature multiseason appeal. Grasses such as silver feather grass (*Miscanthus sinensis* 'Siberfeder'), fountain grass *(Pennisetum alopecuroides)*, and feather reed grass (*Calamagrostis ×acutiflora* 'Karl Foerster') produce fountains of foliage all summer. When they die back, they still provide interesting visual appeal all winter long. Long-lasting dried flower umbels such as those produced by 'Autumn Joy' sedum create architectural interest in the garden in the winter as well. Shrubby *Rosa rugosa* produces cherry-size red hips that offer vibrant color all winter long.

ABOVE Japanese blood grass offers attractive red-tinged foliage. LEFT Hens and chicks are both textural and colorful groundcovers.

Russian sage blooms for several weeks in midsummer.

LONGEST-BLOOMING PERENNIALS

'STELLA DE ORO' DAYLILY (*HEMEROCALLIS* 'STELLA DE ORO')

PURPLE CONEFLOWER (*ECHINACEA PURPUREA*)

ASTILBE (*ASTILBE* SPP.)

COREOPSIS (*COREOPIS SPP.*)

BLANKET FLOWER (*GAILLARDIA ×GRANDIFLORA*)

BLAZING STAR (*LIATRIS SPICATA*)

CATMINT (*NEPETA ×FAASSENII*)

CORAL BELLS (*HEUCHERA SANGUINEA*)

RUSSIAN SAGE (*PEROVSKIA ATRIPLICIFOLIA*)

YARROW (*ACHILLEA MILLEFOLIUM*)

A CATMINT *(NEPETA ×FAASSENII)* offers a dramatic flush of blue blooms in June and again in midsummer. When out of flower, the plant provides handsome mounds of attractive gray-green foliage.

B BLOODY CRANESBILL *(GERANIUM SANGUINEUM)* grows in attractive 1-foot-tall mounded shapes, and it's studded with single-petaled blooms. It flowers in early summer and again in midsummer.

C COREOPSIS *(COREOPSIS VERTICILLATA 'ZAGREB')* is a hardy perennial with fine foliage and sunny yellow flowers.

D SMALL SCABIOUS *(SCABIOSA COLUMBARIA 'BUTTERFLY BLUE')* reblooms after a hard shearing, producing a second wave of frilly-edged blue flowers.

Long-Season Color
Trees and Shrubs

Flowering dogwoods
and sizzling azaleas
turn on the landscape
in early spring.

SHRUBS

Flowering shrubs come in myriad shapes and sizes—and many boost visual diversity by season. Look for shrubs that provide multiseason interest. Serviceberry *(Amelanchier)* offers a lovely upright vase shape in winter. In spring, white petaled flowers create a snowy cloud of bloom, followed by almond-shaped green leaves in summer. Late summer brings purple berries that are edible and attractive to birds. In the fall, the leaves turn a satisfying yellow-orange before dropping to the ground.

Another example of a shrub with full-season appeal is red-osier dogwood *(Cornus stolonifera)*, which grows in full sun or partial shade. The variety 'Argenteo-marginata'

has creamy white flowers for spring appeal. In summer, the leaves sport a white variegated margin. And in autumn, the shrub produces blue-black fruits. But the crowning glory of this shrub is the bright red stems that glow in the fall and winter landscape.

Variegated foliage is also a way to enjoy a color infusion in your landscape. Variegation in plants occurs when a portion of a green leaf is spotted or striped with white, cream, yellow, or pink. This coloration may be on the leaf's edge or in the center.

EVERGREEN TREES AND SHRUBS

Evergreens offer both long-season foliage color and form. Plants such

as yew, juniper, fir, pine, boxwood, and holly wear green foliage all year—and are a welcome sight in areas of the country where deciduous trees drop their leaves in the fall.

Evergreens come in so many types that they are extremely versatile: creeping, weeping, and standard forms all bring different shapes to your landscape. Plus, evergreens respond well to clipping into forms such as squared or rounded hedges. Topiary forms also add elegance and interest to the garden. Evergreens can be clipped into spirals, pom-poms, or cones to accommodate the style of your yard and garden.

A   B   C   D   E

VARIEGATED SHRUBS AND TREES

A VARIEGATED BOX ELDER
(ACER NEGUNDO 'FLAMINGO' PINK)—white and green foliage from spring through autumn

B VARIEGATED GIANT DOGWOOD
(CORNUS CONTROVERSA 'VARIEGATA')—white edges contrast with dark green leaf centers

C JAPANESE EUONYMUS
(EUONYMUS JAPONICA 'SILVER KING')—an upright shrub with dark green leaves edged in creamy white

D WINTERCREEPER EUONYMUS
(EUONYMUS FORTUNEI 'EMERALD 'N GOLD')— a groundcover shrub with attractive green and yellow leaf variegation

E DRAGON'S EYE PINE
(PINUS DENSIFLORA 'OCULUS-DRACONIS')— pine's needles sport horizontal bands of yellow and green

Red-osier dogwood bears bright red branches for excellent winter interest in the garden.

Fast-Growing Plants

Instant gratification has its downside in the garden. Some fast-growing plants fill in fast. But speed may also bring compromise.

Fast-growth trees, shrubs, and plants may sound like the perfect solution when trying to fill in a landscape, but with speed come more maintenance and care.

PROS AND CONS OF FAST-GROWING PLANTS

Any homeowner with a barren, sun-baked front lawn knows the benefits of a fast-growing shade tree. Filling up a landscape fast is the objective of many gardeners—especially those buying a house in a new development where the landscape plantings may start out at 6 inches tall. There are several fast-growing species. For example, you could plant an empress tree and watch it grow 6 to 10 feet in the first year. That's fast. But you may end up dealing with some side effects of fast growth that should be considered before planting a horticultural speed demon.

FAST-GROWTH TREES

Generally, trees grow slowly. But there are species that are faster than others, relatively speaking. For example, the once popular silver maple was widely planted because of its ability to grow quickly and provide shade. This tree is now considered a poor choice for homeowners because its fast growth results in weak wood, which causes the limbs to break easily in windstorms. It also has an aggressive root system that plays havoc with sidewalks or house foundations. The roots can also clog drain and sewer systems. And just when you thought you had enough expensive tree-related repairs, you get the estimate for removing the 50-year-old behemoth from your front yard.

Willows are another example of a popular species that grows quickly. While they provide a lovely tree for home landscapes, willows also drop large and small branches with nearly every gust of wind. When it comes to trees, plant for longevity. Hardwoods such as oak, maple, and hickory grow more slowly, but they cause fewer headaches and last much longer. Medium-fast growing species such as red maple and pin oak are better choices.

CROWD CONTROL

Some otherwise great plants may become aggressive spreaders because they self-seed with abandon. Examples of vigorous self-seeding annuals include spider flower *(Cleome hassleriana)*, violas *(Viola cornuta)*, and love-lies-bleeding *(Amaranthus caudatus)*. Other plants can take over the landscape by simply spreading out. Bamboo is a classic example of a plant that can spread all over unless it's a clumping variety. Bamboos that "run" can become a nightmare beyond your control.

A prime example of an aggressively spreading plant is kudzu vine *(Pueraria lobata)*. It was brought into the southeastern

Fast-growing shrubs can sometimes be too much of a good thing and overgrow the spot they were planted in. Yearly pruning keeps overactive growers in good shape.

**Red Maple
(Acer rubrum)**

United States because of its fast growth to be used as slope-erosion control. An aggressive spreader, it soon became a rampant weed. Another be-careful-what-you-wish-for example is creeping Charlie, the bane of many a lawn lover. Also called ground ivy (*Glechoma hederacea*), it was introduced as a fast-spreading groundcover that loves shady areas.

Garden perennials can also be swift spreaders. Gooseneck loosestrife *(Lysimachia clethroides)*, many mints *(Mentha* spp.), and purple loosestrife *(Lythrum salicaria)* adapt easily to most gardens but will spread in an aggressive manner unless contained or controlled by division. To contain fast-spreading plants, place them in beds with borders that keep them corraled. Or plant them in a bucket with the bottom cut out so their roots can access the earth and water but are unable to spread sideways. Also, do some research before you plant. Many of these aggressive species are illegal to plant in many states.

TREES FOR HOME LANDSCAPES

Choosing trees is an important step in overall landscaping. Here are some popular species with their pros and cons.

FAST GROWING
JAPANESE ZELKOVA (ZELKOVA SERRATA)
Pros: Fast-growing shade tree. Resembles the elm. Low-maintenance. Nice yellow to purple fall color.
Cons: May develop surface roots with age.

BIRCH (BETULA PENDULA)
Pros: Fast growing. Looks great in groups.
Cons: Weakened by drought. Develops surface roots.

WILLOW TREES (SALIX SPP.)
Pros: Fast growth and graceful habit.
Cons: Aggressive roots, weak wood, messy in winds.

TREE OF HEAVEN (AILANTHUS ALTISSIMA)
Pros: Withstands heat and drought. Fast growth.
Cons: Spreads easily. Weak wood.

SYCAMORE/PLANE TREE (PLATANUS ×ACERIFOLIA)
Pros: Very fast growth. Generally deep-rooted.
Cons: Produces litter in the form of seed balls, bark, small branches, and large leaves.

JAPANESE HACKBERRY (CELTIS SINENSIS)
Pros: Fast-growing, spreading tree. Drought tolerant. Wildlife attracting.
Cons: Avoid use near sidewalks; roots cause buckling. Weak trees vulnerable to wind and ice damage.

MEDIUM-FAST GROWING
RED MAPLE (ACER RUBRUM)
Pros: Beautiful red leaves in autumn. Grows in moist areas (also known as swamp maple).
Cons: Doesn't grow well in clay. Prefers rich, acidic soils.

PIN OAK (QUERCUS PALUSTRIS)
Pros: One of the fastest-growing oaks. Mature tree have a very distinctive look—ascending upper branches, horizontal middle branches, and drooping lower branches.
Cons: Requires moist and acidic soils to reach its full growth potential.

GREEN ASH (FRAXINUS PENNSYLVANICA)
Pros: Adaptable to a wide range of soil types (organic, clay, sandy, or rocky) and is extremely tolerant to many types of environmental stresses so it's a good streetside tree.
Cons: Seed litter from female trees.

NOT RECOMMENDED
MULBERRY (MORUS ALBA)
LOMBARDY POPLAR (POPULUS NIGRA)
SILVER MAPLE (ACER SACCHARINUM)
EMPRESS TREE (PAULOWNIA TOMENTOSA)
SIBERIAN ELM (ULMUS PUMILA)

Fast-Growing Plants
Vertical Rocket Plants

Whether you want height for structure, shade, or a privacy screen, there are a number of foliar options that can add instant height to your garden.

Tall plantings can perform many functions in the landscape. They create a sense of enclosure and intimacy. They can help to camouflage an unsightly view or structure. They also serve as great focal points and can make a small yard seem larger by drawing the eye upward.

Many tall-plant options are available. You can buy mature specimens that immediately impact your landscape. Or you can buy smaller plants that grow quickly.

BOLD BARRIERS

You can create a plant barrier—to enclose an area or block a view—with tall columnar-type shrubs such as yew, arborvitae, or privet. For a permanent solution, plant these species in the ground as opposed to containers. They are fast growing and will provide a visual screen as well as a sound barrier from the areas outside your yard. Obviously, the larger the shrub you buy, the greater the screening impact it will have. You can also create a barrier by planting tall shrubs in containers. Many shrubs can live happily in containers provided they are watered and fed on a regular basis and that the container is large enough to allow their roots to grow. By planting a shrub in a large container, you help to elevate it to new heights.

ROCKET PLANTS

There are a number of fast-growing perennials that will gain amazing height in just a season. Tall varieties of ornamental grasses are a great way to add height to your garden. Start with big plants (in gallon-size containers) and plant them directly into the ground or in containers (which makes them immediately appear taller). Tall grass varieties include *Miscanthus sinesis* 'Silberfeder' and the prairie native big bluestem. The tallest perennials include hollyhock (actually a biennial), plume poppy, and perennial sunflower.

**Clumping forms of bamboo add graceful
vertical accents to any landscape. Some
bamboos can grow up to 35 feet tall.**

RISING TO NEW HEIGHTS

Another way to create height in your garden is to give fast-growing vines a leg up. Plant them in containers and train their tendrils on to trellises above their tops to give the illusion of a taller planting. For example, you can purchase a large-sized in-bloom vine such as mandevilla or black-eyed Susan vine, many of which are sold already climbing a support in the pot they are planted in. By gently unwinding the vines from a pot support and training them onto a trellis, you allow them to stretch out.

WHEN TO PLANT SMALL

Avoid planting tall-growing shrubs and perennials where they will eventually obstruct a desirable view, such as in front of a window, near a driveway (where you need to see street traffic to enter the roadway safely), and under power or telephone lines.

Tall-growing shrub species such as arborvitea can create instant impact privacy the same day they are planted.

ROCKET PLANTS

Fast-growing and tall perennials can make a garden seem more established. Try these over-achieving species.

SILVER FEATHER GRASS (MISCANTHUS SINENSIS 'SILBERFEDER')
This ornamental grass grows 6 feet tall and produces white feathery plumes with silky tassels in late August. An excellent choice for a privacy screen, silver feather grass also excels in dried arrangements and offers dramatic winter interest. Another plus—it creates a whispery sound when the wind blows through it. This grass grows best in full sun.

HOLLYHOCK (ALCEA ROSEA)
Reaching 4 to 8 feet high, this biennial is an excellent plant for privacy screens or beautiful vertical accents. It grows best in full sun in deep, rich, well-drained soil. The flowers come in single and double forms in a wide variety of colors from pastels to near black.

PLUME POPPY (MACLEAYA CORDATA)
This perennial has upright stems that reach over 6 feet tall. The plant produces attractive bronze-green leaves and stems are topped with pale pink, feathery flowers. It grows in full sun to light shade and is drought tolerant. Because of its height, it may require staking.

SUNFLOWER (HELIANTHUS SPP.)
This tall-growing plant comes in both perennial and annual forms that reach for the sky—some growing 12 to 15 feet tall. Sunflowers offer bright yellow flowers that are borne on strong stems. Annual sunflowers have large seed heads that feed birds. Perennial sunflowers are hardy and are considered invasive in some areas.

Silver feather grass

Hollyhock

Plume poppy

Sunflower

Fast-Growing Plants
Bulk-Up Plants & Roses

When you have an empty landscape to fill, you want plants that will stand up, spread out, and take over. For fast foliage and bold color, choose plants that will rise to the occasion.

There is a dream team of plants that can accomplish amazing feats of foliar and floral prowess. These plants, known for their ability to spread fast and look great while doing it, are exactly what you need when pondering the possibilities of bare ground.

PLANTS WITH MASS(ING) APPEAL

Some plants can shine as single plantings in the garden. For example, the singular elegance of a Japanese maple makes it better as a solo singer in the garden rather than a member of the chorus. Other plants are more team players—they simply look better in groups. Groundcovers are good examples of plants that work well in a group. Use these low-growing spreaders to carpet an area with wall-to-wall foliage and bloom. Singly, a plant such as vinca minor will send lonely tendrils across the ground. But when planted in snug groups, this vigorous creeper weaves into a verdant groundcover of glossy foliage topped with purple single-petaled flowers.

OPTICAL ILLUSION

By planting the same-colored foliage and flowering plants together, you can create an impression of mass. Blocks of color, such as a bed filled with shoulder-to-shoulder flaming-red celosia plumes, creates a visual experience that not only has a strong presence, but also makes the bed seem larger and more visually important.

CROWDED IN

One way to achieve a uniform mass-planted look is to space annual and perennial flowers close together. The mature dimensions of a plant determine the spacing recommendation listed on a plant tag. To accelerate the coverage, cut the plant tag's spacing requirements in half. For example, if the tag recommends that hostas should be spaced 12 inches apart, plant them 6 inches apart instead. For annuals, close spacing poses no long-term problem. But keep in mind that when you plant perennials closer together than recommended, you may have to dig and divide them more frequently.

BOTTOM LEFT Hydrangeas excel as mass plantings because of their large-headed blooms and attractive dark green leaves. BOTTOM RIGHT Rambling and shrub roses can smother a landscape with color. In summer, they produce fragrant flowers followed by bright orange hips in autumn.

MASS PLANTING DREAM TEAM

GROUND COVERS
Ajuga
Vinca
Pachysandra
Spotted dead nettle

ANNUALS
Petunia
Salvia
Marigold
Zinnia
Portulaca

PERENNIALS
Sedum
Daylily
Gloriosa daisy
Coneflower
Lamb's ears
Chrysanthemum

SHRUBS
Spirea
Barberry
Hydrangea
Dwarf burning bush
Yew
Virburnum

TREES
River birch (for multiple trunks)
Serviceberry
Amur maple
Redbud
Dogwood
Crabapple

RAMBLING ROSES

Both climbing and rambling roses can be used to create mass color and coverage. While climbing roses are more often praised for their vertical feats of coverage, don't overlook rambling roses, which can fill in horizontal areas such as fences and walls with flowers and foliage.

SHRUB MASSING

Flowers are only one type of plant that loves a group mentality. Shrubs can be grouped together to create large beds of beautiful foliage and flower mass. You can use the same species in a grouping of three to five plants. Or you can use multiple complementary shrubs of different heights and colors to create a bold mass of color and texture. For the biggest impact, choose shrub varieties that offer multiple features. For example, 'Gold Mound' spirea produces chartreuse leaves that

ABOVE Use the strength-in-numbers landscaping approach. Small trees planted in a grove makes a bigger statement than a lone tree. ABOVE RIGHT Perennials such as lamb's ears are attractive when planted en masse with roses.

reverberate with electric color in a landscape. Then, in midsummer, this shrub produces rosy-red flower umbels. When planted in mass, this blooming shrub looks like a gorgeous flower garden.

TREE CLUSTERS

Trees can also have mass appeal when you plant them in small clusters or groupings. A grove of trees fills the space with vertical trunks and a canopy of umbrella-like foliage. A tree cluster can be a focal point in a landscape or provide privacy at the end of a property. River birch, serviceberry, and amur maple are tree species that do well growing in a group.

Fast-Growing Plants
Vines on Structures

Perennial trumpet vine envelopes this potting shed with its attractive foliage. Midsummer, this vine produces hummingbird-attracting trumpet-shaped blooms in red, yellow, or orange.

Up, up, and away! Vines are the perfect plants to scramble up and over structures, swathing them with fast foliage and flowers.

It's a perfect relationship: Structure meets vine, and both live happily ever after. Vines, and their wandering ways, soften, romanticize, and sometimes even consume structures in wonderful ways. For example, an unadorned arbor looks lacking without a vine growing over the top. And while the vine enhances the arbor, it also needs it—because of its growth habit, a vine requires a structural support on which to spread out.

Matching the right structure with the right vine is important. For example, a lightweight lattice-type arbor will eventually buckle under the bulk of a woody climber such as trumpet vine. The weighty trumpet vine needs a structure that can hold it up, such as an arbor made of teak or iron. A lightweight wooden or wire structure could more easily accommodate an annual such as cypress vine or cardinal creeper.

There are two basic types of vines: perennial and annual. Perennial vines offer a wide range of colors and bloom times. Popular perennial vines include clematis, wisteria, trumpet vine, and silver lace vine. Woody perennial vines such as honeysuckle, trumpet vine, and grape require heavy-duty supports that can hold up their weight.

Annual vines are fast and fun ways to dress up your landscape in a new color each season. Old-fashioned morning glories are always in style and offer blooms in red, blue, white, purple, pink, and swirly bicolors. Started from seed or planted as seedlings, these assertive growers really take over when the weather gets hot. Other annual vines include sweet pea, moonflower, scarlet runner bean, and hyacinth bean.

Vines that hold special appeal for children include gourds and pumpkins, which can be trained over wire tunnel structures, creating a magical place for kids to learn to garden. Fruit-producing vines that kids love include birdhouse gourds and mini pumpkins.

CLIMBING VINES

Vines are a versatile plant group. They come in both perennial and annual types, as well as both flowering and foliage-only. They can be used to both enhance and disguise the structures that support them.

HYACINTH BEAN (LABLAB PURPUREUS)
A member of the pea family, this easy-to-grow annual vine produces clusters of purple flowers in midsummer. Seed pods follow the blooms and are large, purple, and shiny— very fun! This vine grows 8–12 feet long and is stunning when grown on white picket fences that show off the colorful blooms and seed pods.

CLEMATIS (CLEMATIS SPP.)
These popular perennial vines are adaptable and come in more than 200 varieties. They have spring to fall bloom times and a wide variety of flower types. Clematis does best with about six hours of daily sunlight; keep the lower part of the plant cool by applying a heavy mulch at the base of the plant. Clematis are lightweight vines perfect for small arbors or wooden or wire fences.

CHINESE WISTERIA (WISTERIA SINENSIS)
One of the most beautiful sights in spring is a blooming wisteria vine. This twining, woody perennial produces large, drooping grapelike clusters of purple-blue flowers. This tough vine often climbs high into trees when grown in mild climates. Wisteria is long-lived, and trunks can become quite large and gnarled with age. Wisteria needs a strong support structure.

IVY (HEDERA HELIX)
English ivy is a popular evergreen vine. It's often used as an attractive groundcover. But it is also able to scale brick buildings, stone walls, and fences using aerial roots. The heart-shaped leaves of ivy are dark and shiny and make for a very lush look.

GRAPES (VITIS SPP.)
Grape vines can be a wonderful way to create shade in a pergola. Plus, you have the added value of being able to pluck a ripened cluster of grapes in the autumn. There are many types of grapes you can grow, depending on your zone. Grape vines are heavy, and the fruit adds to their weight, so they must be trained onto a heavy-duty structure.

LEFT Bower vine scrambles across an upside down vintage wire fence.

Hyacinth bean

Clematis

Wisteria

Ivy

Grapes

Fast-Growing Plants
Annual Bedding Plants

Annual bedding plants are the powerhouses of the summer garden. You can buy them in bloom, and they just keep going until cold weather ends their reign in the garden.

If you are looking for constant color companions in the garden, then annual bedding plants are the plants for you. They are an instant impact gardener's dream plant. That's because they are grown for one purpose only—to bloom their little hearts out every day until frost.

Annuals, also referred to as bedding plants, have increased in popularity over the past years. The nearly ubiquitous plants of summer, annuals are used to brighten planting beds in public gardens, parks, shopping malls, office complexes, and other public spaces. Their popularity is due to their ability to add instant color to anywhere they are planted. They are called bedding plants because they are generally planted en masse in a bed to create a large and continuous block of color. They offer a wide range of interesting colors, flower types, and foliage choices. It's probably no surprise that geraniums are the No. 1 bedding plant sold. Runners-up in the competition include impatiens, petunia, marigold, begonia, pansy, salvia, and vinca.

CARING FOR ANNUALS

Annuals are a pretty easy lot, but they do have a few care considerations. They should be planted in well-drained soil. Adding organic material such as ready-to-use packaged garden soil, compost, or well-rotted manure to the soil before planting will ensure that they bloom their best. Because annuals are such flower factories, they appreciate regular feeding during the summer using a balanced fertilizer. While some annuals are more drought resistant than others, most need regular watering to maintain growth and flower production. There are both shade- and sun-loving annuals.

DEADHEADING

You can help many annuals maintain their good looks through deadheading—removing the faded flowers. You can either clip them off with pruners or snap them off with your fingers. When you remove the faded blooms, the plant continues to produce more flowers.

SPACING

The allure of bedding plants is that they grow together quickly into an indistinguishable mass of color. Bedding plants are team players. The more of them you place together, the better they look. When it comes to spacing plants, it all depends on the plant type. But instant impact gardeners can gain a more spectacular look if they space the plants closer together than the plant tags recommend.

EXPERT TIP If you are planting annuals in an area where deer abound, try annual varieties that are more deer resistant: ageratum, calendula, scabiosa, snapdragon, verbena, and zinnia.

Petunias love hot weather and scramble with abandon across the ground, filling in any open space with color.

LEFT Mixing and matching annuals is the best way to have a colorful garden. BELOW RIGHT Ever-blooming annuals—marigolds, zinnias, and dusty miller—add bright spots to this herb and perennial garden.

ANNUALS — FROM SHORT TO TALL

Annuals are one of the largest groups of plant types. From short to tall, you can use these fast-growing, ever-blooming plants in beds, borders, window boxes, and containers.

EDGING OPTIONS

Ageratum—Bright blue frilly blooms offer bold color and unusual flower form.

China pinks—Lacy-edged flowers come in pink, white, red, fuchsia, and bicolors. They have a nice scent too.

Creeping zinnia—A low-growing and prolific bloomer, creeping zinnia offers continuous border coverage in a variety of colors.

Sweet alyssum—Like a lace edge, alyssum offers a softening touch to beds and borders. Classic white is a favorite.

Wax begonia—For shady spots, the begonia flowers bring bold color: pink, fuchsia, red, and white.

Lobelia—The small neon blue flowers of lobelia can be seen from yards away.

Wave™ petunias—These robust growers spread up to 3 feet.

Portulaca—Also called moss rose, these scrappy plants grow almost anywhere, even in the cracks between bricks.

Verbena—Trailing verbena offers large, bright, and colorful flowers that thrive in the heat. Flowers are available in pink, purple, red, and white.

Impatiens—Available in both standard and trailing types, impatiens provide vibrant color in the shadiest areas of your garden. Double impatiens look like tiny roses.

TALL ANNUALS

Angelonia—Also called summer snapdragon, this annual produces orchidlike flowers on lush plants that grow up to 2 feet tall. They love the heat.

Perilla—'Magilla' is a coleus lookalike with foliage shaded with hot pink, green, and deep plum.

Celosia—The stunning flamelike blooms of this annual offer bright color and unusual flower form.

Cleome—Tall, spidery cleome offers airy balls of blooms in pink, dark pink, and white—a must for cottage gardens.

Cosmos—Both the flowers and foliage are winners. The flowers are a simple open petal form, and the foliage is airy and lacy.

American marigold—The stalwart marigold offers sunny color and large multipetaled heads. It's great for seed savers.

Annual sunflower—Available in a wide range of heights, these large-centered flowers feature petals in sunny colors. They're a favorite with birds too.

Zinnia—For cutting or garden color, zinnias can't be beat. They come in candy colors and bloom more productively if cut.

Portulaca	Celosia	Cleome	Marigold

Fast-Growing Plants
Perennials

Perennials are a long-term, beautiful solution to filling your landscape with flowers and foliage. Choosing perennials that are fast growers in the first year means you enjoy instant impact in the garden as well as years of beauty.

When planted in a place they love (correct zone, soil, and light requirements), perennials come back each year, growing bigger and better. Although some species may take longer to achieve their mature size, others seem to almost burst from the ground the moment you plant them.

PLANT FOR BLOOM TIMES
Perennials are on a time-release bloom program. Each species has a specific bloom time. Some flower in the early spring (hellebores, lily-of-the-valley, bleeding heart), midsummer (coneflower, daylily,

sunflower), and others late in the season (aster, mum, boltonia). Some species will even bloom more than once in a season if you shear them back after they finish blooming. But to have a full-season color garden, you need to plant perennials that bloom in every season. This color choreography allows you to enjoy color all season.

BUY BIG AND PACK THEM IN
Spacing perennials closer together can get you a lush look fast. If you buy larger plants (those sold in gallon containers), you can drop already large plants into the ground. By planting them closer together than the plant tag suggests, you can

also create a lusher-looking bed. Mulching between the plants also helps draw them closer together visually so that your bed looks fuller and more mature.

BE CAREFUL WHAT YOU WISH FOR
The old adage "Be careful what you wish for" takes on extra meaning when you plant fast-growing perennials. Plan ahead for their heights, widths, and ability to spread at will. By knowing what to expect when it comes to the assertive (some say aggressive) nature of some species, you can capitalize on their bold and robust ways.

SPEED DEMON PERENNIALS

Fast-growing perennials—wherever growing up or out—offer quick coverage in beds and borders. Grouping these species together en masse creates wide and tall swaths of foliage and flowers.

DAYLILY (HEMEROCALLIS)

This hardy perennial grows fast and generally produces flowers the first season it is planted—especially if you use large, mature plants. The mounding form of the plant is attractive in landscapes, and its grasslike foliage looks good before it blooms. True to its name, the plant produces trumpet-shaped blooms that last one day, then are replaced by new blooms the next day.

RUSSIAN SAGE (PEROVSKIA ATRIPLICIFOLIA)

A very hardy plant, Russian sage grows 3 to 4 feet tall. Covered with long spires of lavender-blue blooms, this woody, sun-loving plant is a fast grower and fills in large areas with its shrubby good looks. The finely cut gray-green leaves have a slight fragrance. This plant tolerates poor soil and is drought tolerant.

MAIDEN GRASS (MISCANTHUS SINENSIS 'GRACILLIMUS')

This is one of the largest ornamental grasses, reaching a height of 6 feet or more each summer. The lovely, arching silvery-green stems are topped with white, fan-shaped flowers. If you don't cut back this perennial after frost, you'll enjoy its mounded upright shape all winter. Maiden grass is an excellent choice for formal beds because of its fine leaf texture and symmetrical form.

PURPLE CONEFLOWER (ECHINEACEA PURPUREA)

This drought-tolerant native wildflower produces masses of purple-pink flowers on sturdy stems. Not only is the perennial a fast grower, it also spreads quickly. Its adaptable nature allows it to excel in full sun and partially shaded locations.

JAPANESE ANEMONE (ANEMONE ×HYBRIDA 'HONORINE JOBERT')

Fast-growing and adaptable to full sun or partial shade, this perennial anemone offers elegant white blooms in late fall. The delicate flowers offer a fringed yellow center surrounded by single white petals with a tinge of pink on the reverse side. Japanese anemone grows best in moist, fertile soil.

SUNFLOWER (HELIANTHUS MULTIFLORUS)

A perennial, this plant grows so fast it may need staking because of its height and general floppiness. It grows up to 5 feet tall and has a clumplike growth habit. The yellow flowers are multipetaled and are excellent for cutting. They look very different from the flat-faced annual sunflower. Perennial sunflowers are sun loving and drought tolerant.

CATMINT (NEPETA ×FAASSENII 'SIX HILLS GIANT')

This hardy and fast-growing perennial creates a lovely mound of blue-green small-leaved foliage that is topped with towering spires of lavender-blue flowers in early spring. If sheared back after bloom, it will flower again later in the summer. A sun-loving perennial, catmint is an excellent edging plant that is attractive to butterflies and bees.

BRONZE FENNEL (FOENICULUM VULGARE 'GIANT BRONZE')

This sun-loving herb creates a tall clump of feathery bronze-purple foliage that is topped with yellow flower heads in mid- to late summer. Fennel is fast growing and works well in borders as a repeated element. The foliage provides a lovely background against which bright-blooming perennials look even better.

Daylily

Russian sage

Maiden grass

Purple coneflower

Japanese anemone

Sunflower

Catmint

Bronze fennel

Roses for Mass Color

Low-growing landscape roses, also called groundcover roses, scramble across the ground with their hardy good looks, recurrent flowers, and glossy green foliage.

Roses are the most beloved flowers in the world, yet some people are a little frightened of growing them. No one has to feel that way about groundcover roses. These low-growing beauties add flair to foundations, cover high-traffic areas with the greatest of ease, and can even stabilize slopes.

FOUNDATION PLANTINGS

Nothing dresses up a house more than a flouncy skirt of blooming roses. And low-growing landscaping roses are the perfect coverup for unattractive cinderblock foundations. They grow 2 to 3 feet tall and spread with vigor across the ground—a rather rosy solution for hiding foundations.

GROUNDCOVER ROSES

Sun-loving landscape roses are excellent choices for beds and borders—and they are especially good choices for streetside plantings because they are hardy and resilient.

ABOVE Groundcover 'Knockout' roses have excellent coverage in the garden. They are tall enough to hide unsightly foundations with their vivid blooms and bright green foliage. **LEFT** Massed 'Flower Carpet' landscape roses create a lovely alley into a garden seating area.

In fact, many landscape roses are used in public landscaping projects for just that reason.

COPING WITH A SLOPE

Landscape roses are also excellent choices for modified slope plantings. Used in areas that are difficult to mow, groundcover roses provide a flowering alternative to grass or other groundcovers. Because they naturally are low-growing, never exceeding 3 feet tall, they offer excellent slope coverage when planted en masse.

LANDSCAPE ROSE CARE

Landscape roses need at least six hours of sunlight a day. They should be watered regularly during dry weather and fed every four to six weeks. Extremely hardy, they require no cover in winter. They are also a good choice for coastal conditions. They rarely need spraying for pests. You can shear off faded flowers to promote additional blooms. In early winter, shear back landscape roses by half.

EXPERT TIP For roses to achieve greatness in both size and flower production, they need regular applications of a slow-release plant food that is high in phosphorus. To keep ever-blooming roses flowering, feed regularly with a water-soluble plant food. Regular feedings will produce better blooms. Another benefit of feeding is that healthy, well-fed plants are also in a better position to fend off pest and disease attacks.

ABOVE LEFT Landscape roses are the perfect solution for a sloped or terraced garden. Mixed with other pastel-hued perennials, they create a bold side yard display. ABOVE RIGHT White 'Flower Carpet' roses planted en masse create a hedge of flowers.

GROUNDCOVER ROSES

'FLOWER CARPET' ROSES include plants that bear white, pink, or red flowers. These roses exhibit high disease resistance, bloom all summer long, and grow about 2 feet tall and 3 to 4 feet wide.

'KNOCKOUT' won the All-America Rose Selection award for best new rose for 2000. It produces clusters of cherry-red flowers throughout the summer and grows 3 feet tall and 3 feet wide. Best of all, it is virtually immune to blackspot.

ROSA 'SCHNEEKOPPE', also called 'Snow Pavement,' produces unusual whitish-lavender flowers that open from purplish-lavender buds. It is a rugosa, which means you can depend on its hardiness. Other pavement series roses include 'Dwarf Pavement' ('Rosa Zwerg') with light-pink flowers and 'Purple Pavement' ('Rotes Meer') with purplish-red blooms.

Lawns

A B
C D

A lush, green, weed-free lawn is every homeowner's goal. Whether you are starting from scratch or upgrading an existing lawn, there are a number of ways to achieve the lawn of your dreams.

Lawns usually contain a combination of grass types. Picking the right mixture for the conditions in your yard is essential. Just as a plant that thrives in dry soil will probably die in a boggy spot, an out-of-place grass will grow poorly or not at all. For example, cool-season grasses prefer a temperature range of 60 to 75° F (16 to 24° C)and generally require less water. Warm-season grasses thrive in higher temperatures (80 to 95° F, 27 to 35° C), but they lose their color when the temperatures drop. Check with your local garden center for advice on the type of grass to plant. Once you've selected the appropriate grass for your area, consider how to plant it.

PREPARATION IS KEY TO SPEEDY SUCCESS

When builders dig a new home's foundation, the soil is dumped on top of the ground surrounding the foundation, burying the topsoil. What many new homeowners end up with for soil is something akin to concrete. The best time to improve the soil is when you are starting a new lawn. So after the lot is cleared of debris and the fine grading has occurred, bring in clean topsoil and amend it with compost.

REPAIR VS. STARTING FROM SCRATCH

It's the 50/50 rule. If your lawn is more than 50 percent weeds, it's more economical (and probably less painful and labor intensive) to start over with new sod than to attempt to fix it. But before you start from scratch, determine what went wrong with your lawn in the first place. Do an assessment asking the following questions:

- Is there shade?
- Is there poor drainage?
- Is there a steep grade?
- What is the soil's pH?
- What is the soil's fertility?

ENLIST THE HELP OF EXPERTS

Have a soil sample taken to determine the best type of grass for your yard. You can process a soil sample through your county extension service, which can offer advice about grass types, new-sod care, and feeding strategies.

LAWN LESSONS

A STAYING IN SHAPE
Proper mowing techniques, feeding, watering, and weeding will keep turf in top shape. Starting with the right grass type for your area means increased success.

B SHADED LAWN
Shaded lawns require special care in order for them to stay as lush and green as the sunny areas of the lawn. To keep healthy grass in shaded areas, mow higher and more frequently. Also, water more often because the tree canopy can shield the ground from rain. Grass that is growing in shade generally is shallow-rooted and less hardy than grass growing in full sun.

C MOWING SENSE
When mowing, cut only a third of the grass blade. You don't need to bag the grass clippings because they do not add to thatch buildup. Mow your lawn in a different direction each time you mow. By altering the mowing direction, you'll get a cleaner cut because the grass blades will grow more erect rather than in a specific direction.

D LESS LAWN
Some homeowners use lawn as a minimalist element in the landscape. They let gardens take up most of the yard, with turf used as the pathway between them. If there are sections of lawn that will be used as pathways, plant a grass type that can stand up to the heavier foot traffic.

COST COMPARISON: SEED VS. SOD

Depending on the variety of grass you select, you can seed a 1,000-square-foot area for about $20. It costs about $200 to sod the same area.

Lawns
Sod and Seed

Sod or seed? Homeowners have two basic choices for creating a new lawn. Sod is nearly immediate, but seed offers a wider selection of grass choices.

If you are looking for the ultimate lawn in a short amount of time, you have two choices. Sod is like installing wall-to-wall carpeting. Start to finish it takes just a couple of hours. Seed is slower, of course, but it is also cheaper and allows you to plant a wider variety of turf types than typically found with sod. Plus, when seeding you can formulate your own seed mixes, which allows you to seed based on the sunny and shady locations of your yard.

Sod for an Instant Lawn

In a couple of hours a team of sod layers can transform your yard into a verdant turf paradise. Here are the steps to sod your yard successfully.

1 CUT OUT THE OLD SOD. Remove existing lawn/weeds by renting a sod cutter to cut and remove the old sod. Calculate the square footage of sod needed (length × width for angular areas or 3.14 × radius squared for circular areas).

2 RAKE THE AREA. Remove debris and smooth out dips and bumps. Keep the soil's level about 1 inch below the surface of sidewalks and driveways so you create a smooth transition between sodded areas and the adjoining pavement. Be sure your yard is prepared before the sod is delivered. Cut sod lasts only about 24 hours when left stacked on pallets.

3 LAY SOD IN ROWS. Tightly butt joints together to prevent the sod's edges from drying out. Use a stair-step pattern to lock the rows together.

4 PRESS OUT LUMPS. Using a sod roller, available at most equipment rental stores, make sure the sod makes good contact with the soil. The roller should be empty when you transport it. When you have it in place on the lawn, fill it with water to give it weight.

5 APPLY A STARTER FERTILIZER. Select a fertilizer with more phosphorus than nitrogen or potassium (20-27-5 is a good choice) to encourage root growth.

6 WATER THE NEW SOD IMMEDIATELY. The grass has just had most of its roots severed when the sod was harvested at the sod farm, so it's important to water frequently to help encourage the growth of a deep root system. Pull up a few corners of sod to be certain water is soaking all the way through as well as an inch or two into the soil below.

SMART BUYER TIP If possible, visit the sod farm to check out the turf's quality in advance of purchase.

Seed—It's Pretty Fast Too

TIME NEEDED 2 to 4 HOURS

Seeding is an economical way to revamp your lawn. Seed offers a wide variety of turf types and many different seed mixtures that are formulated for different types of lawns with different sun/shade situations.

FOLLOW THESE SEEDING STEPS AFTER YOU HAVE REMOVED THE SOD:

1 TILL THE SOIL. Using a gas-powered tiller, till to a depth of 4 inches, add soil amendments such as compost or ready-to-use packaged lawn soil, and till again.

2 RAKE THE AREA. Level the soil and remove debris and remnants of old sod.

3 BROADCAST SEED. Use a spreader to ensure better coverage at the proper rate. A final light raking helps work the seed into the soil.

4 ROLL IT. Rolling the seeded area with a lawn roller helps embed the seeds into the soil. Top with weed-free straw to help conserve moisture, control erosion, and hide the seed from hungry birds.

5 APPLY A STARTER FERTILIZER. Select a fertilizer with more phosphorus than nitrogen or potassium (20-27-5 is a good choice) to encourage root growth.

6 WATER THE SEED. Lightly water the seed (a heavy shower will wash the seeds from their position). Continue to water, not allowing the area to dry out; this may mean multiple waterings per day. Gradually apply more water less frequently to encourage deep-root development. Avoid foot traffic over newly emerging grass.

BUYMANSHIP TIP To ensure you have fresh seed, check the grass seed's current "sell by" date. Look for seed with a germination rate of 85 percent or more, and a weed-to-seed percentage of close to 0.01 percent.

Case Study
Design by Repetition

AFTER!
A barren front yard becomes a foliage fantasy, all with the simple repetition of the same plant—the wonderfully versatile hosta.

PART
#1

1712
SIXTIETH STREET

BEFORE

Landscaping a yard is easy when you start with a good thing—and repeat it. Hosta comes in a wide range of leaf colors, textures, and sizes. Yet this one plant type offers enough variations that it can be used everywhere in the landscape.

Who needs diversity when you have a plant as versatile as the hosta? Available in small edging variations as well as shrub-sized cultivars, the hosta is many plants in one. Plus, larger varieties are often sold in gallon or larger sizes, so you can add robust plants to immediately transform your landscape.

Part One: Front Yard

Once the homeowner gave up the pursuit of the perfect turf, she made this yard more lush and verdant by using a plant that excels in shade. Plus, repetition of the hosta's mounding plant form creates design continuity.

A shaded yard is often a hard place to grow grass. For this homeowner, deep shade was only part of the problem. The other problem was a small landscaping budget. By dividing hostas from the front yard and moving them to the backyard, the industrious homeowner was able to grow her own landscaping stock.

The result: a more verdant and lush-looking yard than grass could ever produce.

Hostas grow best with some morning sun and afternoon shade. Although some varieties will tolerate afternoon sun, plants that are grown in full afternoon sun may experience leaf burn. Some hostas can take a sunnier location. Try 'August Moon,' 'Guacamole,' and 'Sum and Substance.'

HOSTA BLOOMS — COLORFUL AND FRAGRANT

Hostas may be known more for their foliage than their flowers. But many hosta varieties produce some respectable blooms. Flowers range from snow white to dark purple, with all shades in between. If you prefer, you can remove the waving spires of blooms. Hosta's bell-shaped blooms make excellent cut flowers. *Hosta plantaginea* produces one of the most fragrant hosta flowers.

White flower

Purple flower

Lavender flower

Flower bud

Case Study
Design by Repetition

PART
#2

Part Two:
Side Yard

Shaded side yards pose problems for many homeowners. What do you do when grass refuses to grow? Replace it with a shade-tolerant groundcover.

Shady areas offer special gardening challenges. Because they are frequently beneath the overhang of trees, they receive less moisture. In a drought season, this can be especially tough. To help the soil retain moisture, add amendments to the soil, such as sphagnum peat moss, compost, or other organic matter, which also helps keep the soil light and easy to plant in. Mulch around hostas to help preserve soil moisture. And in really dry times, keep shady areas moist using drip irrigation kits or a soaker hose. Always water in the early morning so moisture can evaporate from foliage, thereby discouraging any fungal problems.

In this side yard garden, hostas act as both ornamental shrubs and lawn replacements. Because of their height and width, the larger hosta varieties can function as low-growing shrubs in a landscape plan. And small-stature hostas can replace a less-than-lush lawn. Planting several hosta varieties en masse creates the overall effect of a lush multihued carpet.

The green peace of a hosta garden can be brightened up with other shade-loving plants that produce white foliage or flowers. Both goatsbeard *(Aruncus dioicus)* and snakeroot *(Cimicifuga racemosa)* produce luminous white blooms (and both are tall perennials for back-of-the-border placement). Other white-flowering shade lovers include varieties of astilbe such as 'Weisse Gloria,' columbine such as *Aquilegia vulgaris* 'Crystal,' or meadow rue *(Thalictrum aquilegifolium* 'Alba Florepleno'). For edging, white impatiens can create a footlight effect along paths and borders. Yellow-green planting options include bleeding heart *(Dicentra spectabilis* 'Gold Heart'), golden hakone grass *(Hakonechloa macra* 'Aureola') and spotted dead nettle *(Lamium maculatum* 'Aureum').

Side yards are often problem spots because they are frequently shaded and often too narrow to support any major landscaping. Hostas soften this area into a lush swath of verdant foliage.

SMOOTH leaves are almost glossy and reflect light.

Hostas come in a wide range of sizes and colors, but the growth habit of all varieties is similar—happy little mounds of foliage. A large row of big-leaf hosta camouflages the house foundation while a smaller hosta edges the driveway.

PUCKERED leaves sport a quilted look and hold raindrops like jewels after a rain.

ROUNDED leaves contrast nicely with lance-shape leaves.

POINTED leaves add straplike foliage.

Lusher than lawn, hostas provide ample groundcover from early spring until frost.

CURLY leaves add frilly texture to a shade garden.

PART
#3

PAINT-BY-NUMBER HOSTAS

Hostas come in a number of colors, textures, and leaf shapes. Try these cultivars for a pleasing hosta palette.

VARIEGATED
HOSTA 'SUM AND SUBSTANCE'
HOSTA 'GREAT EXPECTATIONS'
HOSTA 'GOLD STANDARD'

GREEN
HOSTA 'KROSSA REGAL'
HOSTA PLANTAGINEA
'APHRODITE'
HOSTA SIEBOLDIANA
'ELEGANS'

BLUE
HOSTA 'BLUE ANGEL'
HOSTA 'BLUE MAMMOTH'
HOSTA 'HALCYON'

Part Three:
Back Yard

Hostas offer shade gardeners a wide range of leaf shapes, textures, and colors.

With more than 2,500 hosta varieties on the market today, it's unsurprising that this plant has so many different looks. Hostas are one of the easiest perennials to divide. In the early spring, just after the plant has sprouted leaves, use a sharp spade to lift the entire plant from the ground. Using a serrated knife, cut the plant in half, thirds, or more pieces, depending on the original size of the plant. Replant each piece in new locations.

A RIVER OF FOLIAGE A meandering line of variegated hostas creates the illusion of a stream bed in this side yard garden.

B ON THE EDGE Edging a bed of hostas with more hostas is a bold move, but it works because of the diversity of the leaf types. The edging hostas feature dark green spearlike leaves that contrast nicely with the lighter green hostas in the bed.

C HOSTA MEDLEY Using the same basic plant but altering its look by planting different sizes and leaf colors creates a sense of uniformity and order in this small space.

D FENCE-LINE FRINGE Large hostas can be used as shrub replacements in narrow spots. By alternating the leaf forms and colors of the hosta varieties, you can create a patchwork foliage effect.

E REPEAT TO COMPLETE Large-leaved hostas are the perfect groundcover because of their size. Massing large hostas in a small area creates continuity through repetition of the same plant.

CHAPTER FIVE

PUTTING IT ALL TOGETHER

Good design is the fastest way to achieve an instant garden. And the design doesn't have to be elaborate in order to look great. In fact, simple garden elements are often the most impactful.

In this chapter...

Design Overview

Every great garden starts with a plan. Garden plans don't have to be complicated or even drawn up by a professional. The secret is to create a plan of action that results in outdoor living spaces that reflect your lifestyle.

Whether you are creating a landscape plan yourself or hiring a professional, it's smart to understand the basic design elements before you begin. The best landscape plans emphasize simplicity and unity of design.

GETTING STARTED

Assess your garden's weak and strong points. Is there a beautiful shade tree in the corner of the property that you want to emphasize and incorporate into the landscape design? Think about how you use your landscape. Are you looking for a meditative retreat after a stressful week at work? Or is your backyard a place where you entertain family and friends?

As you answer such questions, you'll begin to develop a vision of what you'll need to do to reach your goals.

And finally, the big question is: Can you accomplish what you want by adding to your landscape, or will you need to start over from scratch?

KEEP IT SIMPLE

Landscapes that have the biggest impact are often the simplest in design. A single focal point, such as a rustic arbor covered with vining roses, a trickling fountain surrounded by fragrant herbs, or a

ABOVE LEFT Repeating a shape or motif allows you to create a sense of unity in the garden. Landscape design by Fletcher Steele. LEFT Creating a unified look among structures and plantings is important in creating an overall and consistent design.

piece of antique artwork at the end of a garden path, is often all you need to transform a mundane backyard into an exciting experience.

Often the less complicated you make a garden plan, the easier it is to fulfill and the more impact it provides.

UNIFY TO SIMPLIFY

Good garden design unifies the elements of your landscape. Paths, beds, and structures all create a sense of order and purpose, so their relationship in the landscape is important.

It's a good idea to plan the unity of your garden around its use. If your garden is the place where you go to sit, relax, and unwind, then add elements that meet those needs (seating, a water garden, a flower bed of fragrant plants). If your yard and landscape are used by the whole family, their design should fit the needs of children, adults, and pets. Therefore, it's important to create separate areas for play, entertaining, and enclosure, and it's crucial to create a sense of unity among them.

A good way to impose unity on your outdoor spaces is to think of them in the same way that you do the inside of your home. Every room has a purpose, and rooms are arranged based on their uses. Your outdoor areas have the same design needs. Even a small area such as a tiny side yard can be made both beautiful and useful.

Another important way to unify the landscape is with color. Working within a particular palette, you can add outdoor cushions, painted furniture, and plant selections to help visually tie together the various corners of your landscape. One instant way to bring it all together with color is to select pots and planters of a particular color palette and to place them throughout the landscape as unifying elements.

Plants, especially bold-colored annuals in the same color palette, also can be planted in large drifts or clumps to add drama to the yard and give the impression of a grand and unifying plan.

Controlling the View

A B

C D

If your yard were a painting, what element would draw your eye in? Creating a focal point in garden design is all about choosing a star and making everything else in your yard a supporting player.

By its very definition, a focal point is the place where your eye goes first. A focal point catches your attention and draws your eye to look near or far. It may be the largest, brightest, or most prominent feature of the yard. For example, an attractive flower-covered bower or a piece of art in the center of a garden bed are desirable focal points. But effective focal points can also be subtle manipulators, such as the curving shape of a garden path or the bold use of color.

CONTROLLING THE VIEW

The purpose of good garden design is to control the view using an object or series of objects that you choose and place. And it's as much about what you don't see as what you do. Focal points can draw the eye away from the less-desirable aspects of a landscape. An effective focal point creates an immediate sense of order in a yard. It also creates a sense of purpose and even correctness in the landscape.

STRUCTURES

An architectural element in the garden, such as a pergola, arbor, arch, or gateway, creates an instant impact focal point. Swathe it in flowering vines such as climbing roses, wisteria, or clematis, and you heighten its beauty and romance.

INVITING PATHS

A walkway or path has the dual purpose of providing a visual line of sight and a physical map of where to go next. Capitalize on the already visually controlling concept of a path by placing a focal point or resting spot at the end of the path. A bench or piece of art, such as a sculpture or sundial, may provide exactly what is needed to bring the eye down to the path's end.

SHOW-STOPPING SPECIMENS

You can create a focal point in your garden by adding one special and dramatic plant or group of plants. For example, adding a tall flowering tree rose in the center of a bed of low-growing annuals creates a focal point by scale. The taller plant naturally draws the eye to it because of its relative size. In fact, placing a tall plant in the center of a bed is more dramatic than placing it at the back of the bed.

CREATIVE COLOR

Color is another simple way to create a focal point. Any dramatic color change will attract attention. For example, in a shade garden, white-blooming or light-colored foliage will draw the eye to it—simply because of the contrast. Bold color, such as a saturation of a single color (all red flowers, all blue flowers) also makes a dramatic yet subtle focal point.

GARDEN VIEWPOINTS

A FRAMED VIEW
Using the natural, arching growth habit of trees and shrubs, you can direct the view. Here, columnar crabapple trees stand sentry at a garden entrance, framing the sunlit entryway with shadow and foliage. The layered focal point of the bench and the standing structure beyond draws the eye into the garden.

B STEP INSIDE
Garden gates are both physical and visual ways to offer an invitation into a garden or yard. The decorative nature of this gate makes it especially appealing. The large post-capping finials offer style-setting architectural interest.

C ARCH RIVALS
Arched structures create a view-finder effect, like a photo being composed. Used in a series (as in the repeated arch here), they create a sort of "tunnel vision" that moves the eye to the point at the end, which best culminates in an eye-stopping focal point such as planter or bench.

D ART TO GAZE AT
A piece of garden art—a statue, column, or whimsical sculpture—makes an effective focal point. Placed in the center of a bed or border as a lone object, it draws the eye. Formal gardens use garden art sparingly but effectively. For example, in the center of a parterre bed, an armillary, obelisk, or tuteur is often the focal point.

A mature allée offers an arched canopy of foliage as well as the pleasing vertical elements that the tree trunks provide. The symmetry of an allée draws the eye to the end—like a tunnel.

Plant an Allée

Creating a focal point is easy when you direct the view with an allée that can be planted in an afternoon.

Nothing directs the eye more effectively than a set of parallel lines. And that is exactly what an allée is—a sort of horticultural parallelogram. Traditionally, allées were used as formal design elements, lining both sides of a path or driveway. With plants lined up and facing one another across the path, the ultimate goal of an allée is for the plants to grow large enough so that their canopies touch and enclose the pathway in a private foliage tunnel.

This design element, however, can be used effectively in any type of garden. And, you can alter the more formal element of an allée garden by using less formal plantings. In English gardens, the traditional trees for allées are linden, oak, or beech. But any tall, somewhat columnar tree or shrub can be used.

Large trees or shrubs are just one way to produce an allée effect. You can plant tall upright perennials to achieve a similar look. The placement and repetition of plant material creates a softer, less formal allée. Good perennials to use for this type of allée are tall grasses. A more airy and ephemeral allée might be two facing narrow borders of *Verbena bonariensis*. Or you could alternate plantings with structural elements, such as stone pillars, to get the same sort of effect.

TIME NEEDED
4 to 6 HOURS

HOW TO PLANT A FOCAL-POINT ALLÉE

1 LAY OUT THE AREA for the allée, using stakes and string. Ideally, the allée should be located on a flat surface.

2 SELECT A PLANT/TREE species suitable for the area.

3 SET THE POTS the length of the allée, based on the spacing requirements of the allee plants, making sure to line up the plants across the path from one another.

4 DIG A HOLE for each tree and plant.

5 PLACE A FOCAL POINT at the end of the pathway.

ALLÉE TREE OPTIONS

Flowering trees, such as crabapples, pears, and cherries, are especially nice choices for allées because of their multiseasonal color show—snowy petals in spring; glossy green foliage in summer; and small fruits (on fruiting varieties) in autumn.

CRABAPPLE
(MALUS SPP.)
This small ornamental is perfect for backyard or side yard allées. Dwarf varieties, such as the Sargent crab (*Malus sargentii*) offer smaller options.

CRAPE MYRTLE
(LAGERSTROEMIA INDICA)
Blooming in a range of colors, crape myrtle varieties also come in many heights.

FLOWERING DOGWOOD
(CORNUS FLORIDA)
A white-flowering understory tree, this dogwood grows about 30 feet tall with elegant spreading branches.

LINDEN
(TILIA AMERICANA)
Linden trees, also called basswoods or lime trees, are the classic choice for a traditional allée. They exhibit a natural pyramidal shape that requires little pruning. They produce small, round fruits and the leaves are golden yellow in autumn.

Controlling the View
Create a Vista

An Outdoor Wall Offers a Two-Way View

BEFORE

AFTER!

AFTER!
A corrugated tin wall screens a work area. Unusual building materials such as corrugated metals allow you to introduce new looks and textures to a landscape.

1

2

3

4

5

TIME NEEDED
2 to 4 DAYS

A wall with windows controls the view in several ways: It hides a work area and creates a secret vista from three open-air windows.

You can create the view you want in your yard with two powerful design tools: disguise and re-direction. By erecting a wall to disguise a work area in front of a barn, the homeowners also re-directed the view. The new view is a reflective wall made from corrugated tin, a low-maintenance garden bed planted with fountainlike grasses, and three open-air portholes that allow visual access from the yard to the work area. The creative chaos of the work area behind the wall is shielded from view. The Southwestern-inspired garden is planted with low-maintenance grasses, mulched with gray stone, and edged with black plastic to create an easy mowing path around the area.

1 MARK OUT THE AREA. Measure the area for a wall and mark it off with stakes and spray paint. Anchor the posts of the wall in concrete to create stability (the posts are sunk into concrete footings).

2 BUILD THE FRAME. Based on the dimensions of your yard, determine the length and height of the wall. Work with a lumberyard to determine the dimensions of the posts, frame, and window trim needed for your design. Use pressure-treated lumber, especially anywhere where the wood comes in contact with the ground. This frame is built in four segments—three of which feature a window.

3 ATTACH THE TIN. Using zinc plated or stainless steel sheet metal screws, attach the sections of corrugated tin to the frame sections.

4 TRIM THE WINDOWS. Create a framed-in window using miter-edged trim. Paint the trim a contrasting color if desired.

5 TOP WITH STONE. In keeping with the Southwestern theme, balance round river stones on top of the wall. The juxtaposition of contrasting textures and mediums (tin and stone) is a surprising element.

6 MAKE A BED. A curved planting bed snugs up to the angular walls. Planted with low-care, drought-tolerant grasses and mulched with gray gravel, this bed is marvelously minimalist.

7 ENJOY THE VIEWS. The windows provide visual access from the yard to the work area.

Like a camera's viewfinder, this window frames a specific view—a peaceful fountain still life.

151

A B
C D

When designing your garden, be open to making some bold moves. Color, structure, and planting techniques can be combined to create a dramatic and memorable landscape.

Boldness is in the eye of the beholder. What is a bold concept to one person may seem tame to another. And because gardening is a personal expression, being bold is entirely up to the taste and aesthetics of the gardener. There are a number of design tools you can use to transform your landscape into a one-of-a-kind personal statement.

BE BOLD YOUR OWN WAY

In order to create a bold look in your garden, you need to define what bold is to you. Is it a dramatic use of color? Is it following the specific style tenets of an established garden design, such as the symmetry of formal gardens, the impressionistic color palette of country gardens, or the minimalist simplicity of a contemporary style? Or are you less interested in the historic echoes of garden design but yearn to express your own personal vision?

COLOR

Color is one of the simplest ways to increase the boldness in your garden. Not only do plants supply color (and in great numbers, the color intensity can create boldness), but you can also infuse color through artificial methods of your own making, such as with paint and fabric. The boldness of color depends on how you use it and the contrast that is created. For example, in an all-green hosta garden, a swath of bright-blue Virginia bluebells adds bold color in the shade in spring. Yet in a blazing blue bed of 'Victoria' salvia, a restful edge of white creeping zinnias creates the bold contrast.

STRUCTURE

Nothing commands the limelight in a garden like structure. A wall, an arbor, a folly—all these added components are the human elements around which a garden grows. Adding structure to your landscape can serve bold purposes. It offers a sense of scale and a sense of design style even though most structures are wholly utilitarian—creating enclosure or offering space for storage or a place for seating.

ACCENTS

Garden accents are the most personal expressions. They may represent adherence to a specific garden style, such as a sundial in the middle of a formal bed or a beehive in an herb garden. Although most people no longer tell time using the sun or gather honey from their own gardens, these accents represent a decorative nod to garden tradition—and the recognition of a time when gardens were utilitarian as well as decorative. Garden accents also allow gardeners to express themselves artistically through the placement of statuary, abstract art, or self-created objects of beauty.

GARDEN DRAMA

A FLYING COLORS

Using both color and structure, this post-and-banner pergola creates a sense of drama in the landscape. Both temporary and permanent structures can raise the excitement level in a garden.

B THREE IN A ROW

Boldness can be achieved in the simplest ways. An unusually shaped container is bold. But replicating the look times three is even bolder. Repeating an element in the garden or landscape allows you to create a sense of order and excess that makes a bold statement.

C SIZZLING COLOR

Color is one of the best ways to express yourself boldly in the garden. A large saturation of color, either on a wall or as a planting group, draws the eye. Color adds an emotional element to the garden. Bright colors are active. Pastel colors and shades of green offer a more restful feeling.

D STUNNING STRUCTURES

Even smaller or less elaborate structures can make a statement in the landscape. Depending on the style of garden, you may incorporate modern or traditional structures.

Bold Landscaping
Color

A cobalt blue wall is the perfect backdrop for the hot pink bougainvillea. After the blooms fade, the wall's color continues to add drama to the garden.

Color may be the most important feature (and quickest to add) in a garden because of its immediate effect on the eye—and the emotions.

There are many ways to infuse color into your landscape. Flower and foliage allow you to paint your landscape with all the colors that nature has created. And paint and fabric allow you to color your garden with the pigments that humanity has created. With such diverse palettes, it's good to have a sense of what you want to do with so much choice.

PURSUING A PALETTE

There is some order in how colors are expressed. Primary colors are red, yellow, and blue. These colors (and their shades) are the basis for the creation of all other colors. Colors organized on a color wheel allow you to choose the colors that go best together. The secondary colors on the color wheel are orange, green, and violet.

When you combine colors in the garden, you can do one of two things. You can match colors that harmonize based on their position on the color wheel. Or you can use contrasting colors.

ONE-COLOR GARDENS

To achieve a monochromatic color scheme, you select one color and use various shades of it in the garden. For example, if you were planting a blue garden, you'd need to choose species and varieties that produced blue, purple, or lavender flowers or foliage. This planting

scheme creates a restful and pleasing effect that is also simple to execute. In a monochromatic garden, plant height and texture take on more important roles. The trick of this garden design is to create subtle juxtapositions of plantings. Some gardeners may find it boring to use only one color for all flowers, but within that one color, there is a huge range of plant options. And although this color scheme seems simple (and it can be), its simplicity can mask interesting complexities that intrigue many gardeners.

COLOR COUSINS

When you work with analogous colors, you have a palette that gives you more flower and foliage options than a monochromatic garden. A good example could be a hot-colored border containing a variety of red, yellow (primary colors), and orange (the secondary color that is created when you combine red and yellow). This color scheme is easy to create because these color cousins look good together naturally.

HIGH CONTRAST

If you want maximum color impact, select colors that are opposite each other on the color wheel. For example, contrasting color pairings would be yellow/purple, orange/blue, and red/green. Because no hue is common to these pairings (like the relationship of red, yellow, and orange), the impact is most dramatic.

GOING ALL THE WAY

For gardeners who want the exuberance that all the colors of the rainbow bring, the polychromatic color scheme is the way to go. All colors are fair game, and the trick to this type of gardening is to create pairings that are pleasing to the eye rather than chaotic. An informal cottage-style garden is a good example of this type of color scheme in action.

ABOVE LEFT Grouping different plants of the same color creates a monochromatic garden that dramatically draws attention to plant textures. Here, yellow and green are the dominant colors.
ABOVE A garden bed packed with autumn crocus is ablaze in fall bloom.

EXPERT TIP
The use of color is one of the best ways to create emotion in your garden. Determine the feel you want for your garden, then plant varieties that bloom in cool colors for a calming effect and hotter hues for a sense of excitement and exhilaration.

Bold Landscaping
Accent

A modern bottle tree makes a garden-appropriate accent.

An elegant copper fountain is surrounded by balls of barbed wire.

Every garden—just like the gardener who plants it—has a distinct personality. Make your garden as individualistic as you are by infusing it with bold accents of your own personality.

Your garden can be a true reflection of yourself. The accents that you choose help define the space as your own—showing your interests, sense of humor, and whimsical view of the world. After all, a garden is your little piece of the world—the place that you create—so infuse it with your own personality.

BE BOLD, HAVE FUN

Look around your garden to find places where you can introduce whimsy and fun. For a little literary humor, position a sedentary stone tortoise next to a fast-growing hare topiary in homage to the famous Aesop fable. Or place a sundial in an herb garden bed of thyme for a play-

ADDING HUMOR TO YOUR GARDEN

Let your sense of the absurd be your guide when appointing your garden with art and artifacts.

PINK FLAMINGOS—Classic kitsch, these standard fuchsia-pink yard ornaments have been standing in gardens for nearly half a century.

GNOMES—Traditional English garden ornaments, gnomes in their festive red pointed hats are small enough to stand guard in any garden.

REPEATED SHAPES—Interesting abstract sculpture can be made by repeating common objects: gears, heads, hands, birdhouses.

SCARECROWS—A scarecrow made from castoff garden pots looks like a terra-cotta slinky toy.

WEATHER VANES—Used on the tops of houses and barns to show which way the wind blows, these decorative pieces make excellent ornamentation in gardens.

ARCHITECTURAL ARTIFACTS—Doorways that serve as arbors, doors that lead to nowhere, windows looking out over the garden, mirrors reflecting the view, pediments, and other architectural bric-a-brac—they all add surprisingly traditional echoes when used in the garden.

on-words joke (it's time for thyme).

Get more outrageous by working within a theme. If you love old birdhouses, gather a flock of your favorites and erect them on posts of varying heights in your garden beds. Where one birdhouse would be simply utilitarian, an excessive number of them becomes fun. The sum of their parts becomes whimsical art.

INDULGE YOUR LOVES

Surround yourself in your garden with what you love. If you fancy fairies, position them amid the beds and borders. If you love butterflies, decorate the garden with their images (and make sure you also plant nectar-rich flowers so you can attract the real thing). Here's the rule for bold garden accents: If you like it and it makes you smile, it's good.

CREATE YOUR OWN ART

An old-fashioned bottle tree is a great way to add light, color, and form—along with a healthy helping of whimsy—to the garden. Use a dead tree with slender branches or a man-made structure and cover it with bottles. Bottle trees were used long ago in the South with the idea that their reflective colors warded off evil spirits. Today, a brightly colored bottle tree is more likely to invite good-natured people into the garden.

CLEAN OUT YOUR ATTIC

Old furniture in the garden is also a way to add familiar elements used in unfamiliar ways. For example, an old iron headboard and footboard, planted with a blanket of sleep-inducing chamomile is a fun way to use a retired antique in the garden. A wooden ladder-back chair with flowers growing up through the

missing seat makes art out of a castoff. Even an old bicycle, its metal kissed with rust and intertwined with a morning glory vine, can add whimsy to a garden bed.

SURPRISE YOURSELF

Traditional garden art can be used in surprising ways. Statuary, both naturalistic and impressionistic, can be placed in traditional positions such as at the end of a path as a focal point. Or art can be furtive and secretive, such as a toad garden ornament seated beneath a low-growing hosta leaf—to be discovered by only the occasional passerby as an intimate inside joke. Let art imitate life in the garden—perch a stone bird on top of a picket fence slat. Or position an inscrutable stone cat at the edge of a koi-filled water garden.

Bold Landscaping
Architecture

Adding architectural elements is a design principle used in traditional gardens. But structure can play a role in fun and nontraditional ways too.

Y ou need to think big when using architectural elements in the garden. Larger and more imposing than garden ornaments, architectural elements can serve two purposes: as large focal points and as places to inhabit. Common garden architecture includes follies, gazebos, colonnades, and arches. Consider installing an architectural element that supports and enhances your garden's style.

FUN WITH FOLLIES
Traditional English gardens employed structures called follies to adorn a large garden. These structures may have been other-than-functional buildings (some were built to look like a building but lacked any door of entry). But they provided a focal point or anchor at the end of a garden. Usually designed to reflect the style of a specific period (Greek revival, Romanesque, Georgian), a folly was a focal point as well as a destination in the garden. Some were

ABOVE Architecture defines the style of the garden. This modern seating area sets the tone for the rest of the garden.
LEFT Architecture can transcend the utilitarian. Here, three walls create a focal point for a garden.

whimsical—for example, a building in the shape of a giant pineapple. Follies are still used in modern gardens. These small buildings can be great places from which to enjoy the garden: a teahouse, a decked-out playhouse for children, or an off-site studio for writers, artists, or dreamers.

GAZEBOS

These open-air buildings are both a strong structural focal point in the landscape and a great place to host parties and dinners. Like follies, they also offer a destination in the garden. Because gazebos are roofed, they offer a shady respite on sunny days or shelter from a gentle rain shower. Designs range from popular Victorian styles with gingerbread and other decorative bric-a-brac to more rustic retreats. Some gazebos can be updated for multiseason use. For example, a ceiling fan in a gazebo keeps the air moving and the mosquitoes away on hot summer nights. And some gazebo kits come with

screened sides so that the structure can be used from early spring through late autumn.

POTTING SHEDS

Potting sheds are the poor man's folly—hardworking structures that can look upscale. These buildings, made to house tools and garden machinery, can be as ornate as you want. While the inside of a potting shed effectively holds all the materials and tools needed to create a great garden, the outside can disguise the utilitarian purpose. There are a variety of garden-shed plans or kits that can mimic the style of your home. The kits are easy to assemble and can be modified with paint and other decorative enhancements to create a unique building that serves as an architectural enhancement in your yard.

COLUMNS AND ARCHES

As a mere remnant of a structure, a column is a historical placeholder in the landscape. It suggests history, but without the structure, weight, and

follow-through. Columns are perfect focal points and can serve as pedestals for plantings, or they can stand alone without adornment. They come in many styles—from scrolled Greek columns to stone-stacked prairie-style columns. Like columns, arches also incorporate architectural elements without the building attached. Arches represent a portal from one place to another. An archway in the garden suggests other spaces—other gardens. In other words, an arch creates the illusion of continuing space.

COLONNADES

A colonnade is a series of columns and a very effective way to create a linear, moving focal point. Echoing Greek and Roman architecture, a row of columns creates a classical look wherever it is placed, regardless of whether the columns are classical in design. Positioned in a row, columns offer an airy, roofless structure that can define a landscape.

Less Is More

A B
C D

Simplicity can be your best friend in garden design. A "less is more" attitude can help you keep your design decisions simple, quick, and doable.

It's a good idea to do a visual assessment of your landscape every few years. Like the inside rooms of your home, your garden and landscape can lose design focus over time. It's inevitable that you accumulate new garden possessions such as furniture and accessories. And if you add new plants to the garden, containers to your patio, or window boxes to your home's exterior, you are adding to the abundance—and possible clutter—of your landscape.

Not only should you assess your garden additions—the ones you bring in yourself—but you should also review the plants in your garden. As plants mature, they can outgrow their position in the landscape. The same bare backyard that you filled with planting beds five or 10 years ago may have become an overgrown jungle.

Every healthy landscape evolves. Young saplings grow into trees that can turn a once-sunny backyard into a shady woodland. Beds that once housed sun-loving perennials may now be in full shade—with plants that are starved for light. A verdant lawn can become a threadbare expanse once tree canopies have filled in and shaded the grass.

REDUCE VISUAL COMPLEXITY

The best way to simplify your landscape is to reduce its visual complexity. Start with the stuff you can physically pick up and move. Take everything but the plants out of your garden. Does it look too barren? If so, add back a table, a bench, a pot. Keep adding back elements until your landscape has the look you want—less cluttered, more streamlined, more to the point.

ELIMINATE CLUTTER

Next, review the plantings. Do perennials need dividing? Do shrubs need pruning? Do tree limbs need thinning? Are there plants that need to be removed entirely because they no longer fit the space? Determine what you can do with pruners, loppers, and a small chain saw to reduce the visual complexity of your plantings.

MAINTAIN THE THEME

A good garden design stays true to its overall theme. This is the governing design concept that helps you stay on track. If your garden is formal, is it still meeting the elements that define that style? If your goal was to create an abundant old-fashioned cottage garden, is the garden meeting its objectives or has it become an unruly mess? It's your garden, and you decide how you want it to look. But remember, a garden is always changing in nature and will continue to evolve. It's your job to keep it on track with your original vision.

SCALE BACK

A CREATING A VIEW
Looking at your landscape from all angles allows you to see the beauty in simple things. For example, some homeowners might consider trimming back the arching limbs on this tree to open up the view. But to others this natural element frames and enhances the view, creating balance and unity in the landscape.

B SIMPLE IS BEAUTIFUL
Simplicity in the garden is all about identifying a strong element of design and allowing it to perform in the landscape. For example, a simple walkway lined with trees allows the eye to move down the path unrestricted, creating a sense of movement and balance.

C LAWN ORNAMENTS
An expanse of lawn becomes a work of art when simple stone elements are added. Natural and asymmetrical, these stones create a sense of order and place in an otherwise empty landscape.

D GRASS SWATHS
Simple in design and maintenance, this landscape is created from alternating widths of low-growing evergreen shrubs and ornamental grasses. By adding the beds of wheat-colored grasses, this landscape acquires both color and texture to add visual interest, all done with the simplest of designs.

Less Is More
Lawn as Minimalist Art

Your lawn can make a small and quiet statement when it becomes minimalist art rather than a great green carpet. And less lawn means less maintenance.

The love of a lawn can be traced to European tradition. Large expanses of green grass surrounded estates and villas, making the architecture look grand—like a giant ship on a sea of rolling turf. Today this tradition continues, with large lawns being the norm in neighborhoods, where they roll out from the front door and don't stop until they meet the street.

A lush lawn is a wonderful thing. The thrill of all that green is undeniable. A great-looking lawn makes everything it surrounds—trees, shrubs, flowers, your home—look better because it serves as a foil—a background that shows everything in contrast.

But there are new and exciting ways to look at lawns—and you can still get a big-bang lawn with less. A lawn doesn't have to command all the space around your home. In fact, a minimalist lawn can capitalize on all the aspects of a grand, rolling lawn—the great green color, the soft bouncing feel when you walk barefoot across it, the coolness that it imparts both visually and in temperature. You can have less grass and still enjoy its benefits.

ABOVE LEFT A turf pathway links gardens. LEFT A turf platform raises basic grass to a new level as a design element.

LEFT Even a small lawn can benefit from turf's great looks. Islands of grass can offer a verdant feel without the expanse or expense of a large lawn. BELOW A grass-and-brick checkerboard provides the softening effect of lawn without the summer-long mowing commitment.

LAWN AS STAGE

If what you love about a green lawn is an expanse of cool, calm green, you can still have that look, but with a limited run. Turfgrass (bottom left) can be planted on an elevated platform—like a second layer on a cake—to create a stage of green. Smaller than a traditional lawn, the platform is elevated in stature by raising it a mere 5 inches from the ground. Its height and compact size set it apart from other lawns, and thereby make it special. It becomes finite—it has a beginning and an end. The square of lawn works rather like an area rug inside a home. It defines the space and makes it more intimate.

TURF SQUARES

Even with a smaller amount of turf, you can still enjoy its good points. You can cut your turf's surface area by half and still reap all its benefits. By alternating grass squares with equal-size concrete or stone you can cut your lawn chores in half—while imparting a new and interesting look. An alternating turf and stone checkerboard allows you to have the calm respite that turf offers as well as solid areas to hold furniture or art.

GRASS ACCENTS

The grassy feel (the green blades, the soft look) can be retained when you use turf as an accent rather than a blanket effect. When you create planting areas around patios and terraces, you have the calming look of grass without a vast lawn. You can plant grass seed in soil pockets, or you can cut sod into the shapes you need, then insert it into the areas. Small lawn pockets such as these can be cared for with less intensive lawn care techniques, leaving you more time to enjoy your green spaces.

CUTTING SOD IN SHAPES

Working with a strip of sod is like working with cookie dough. Rolled out, it can be cut into a variety of shapes to be used in creative ways. For sod, simple shapes that maintain a good root area are the easiest to cut and maintain. Here are tips to help you cut sod to fit a scheme for your minimalist lawn.

1 DETERMINE THE SHAPE you want; use a pattern to cut sod if necessary.

2 USE A SERRATED TOOL, such as a sod cutter or a knife.

3 POSITION THE SOD shape onto well-watered soil.

4 WATER WELL—soak to the roots.

Less Is More
Design by Removal

BEFORE

A Woodland Room

TIME NEEDED
1 to 2 DAYS

Removing elements of your yard are a fast way to reveal hidden treasures of space and use. By deleting scrubby trees at the overgrown end of a lot, this homeowner carved out a woodland hideaway.

AFTER!
An overgrown yard becomes an intimate seating area with simple removal and reshaping techniques.

Much of garden design is centered around the addition of things—structures, beds, borders. But equally important is the ability to subtract from your yard to reveal and clarify new areas and uses. And subtraction is the fastest way to make a big impact in your yard.

DO THE MATH

How do you know when to subtract elements from your landscape? If you want more room in your yard, if an area is overgrown, unattractive, and unused, or if your space seems too confined, then it might be time to remove some elements. Subtracting elements from a landscape can add a new dynamic to your yard.

SCULPT SPACE

The most obvious place from which to subtract is an area of a yard that is overgrown. For this homeowner, the subtraction area was easy to identify: An overcrowded clump of conifers at the end of the property was unappealing and made the space unusable.

The first step to subtracting elements in the landscape is to figure out how far to go. Since tree removal is an irreversible act, take it slow. Remove one tree and stand back and survey the look. If you need to remove more, do it tree by tree, with inspection intervals in between. By removing several trees and saplings, this homeowner carved out an area that was large enough to accommodate two willow love seats—the perfect furniture choice for a sylvan retreat.

CREATE A NICHE

Once the area was cleared, the remaining trees let in too much light, making the seating area feel a bit too open. To enclose and define the area, the homeowner used plastic ties to lash several newly cut tree saplings to existing trees to create a natural semicircle picket fence that surrounded the seating area. Additions to the rustic enclosure include old Christmas trees.

DECK IT OUT

Defined by nature, this rustic hideaway is outfitted with some important elements of comfort. The seats of the willow pieces are topped with comfortable red bench cushions. Patchwork and striped woven throw pillows add surprising flashes of color. Rescued from the woodpile, various-sized tree chunks are put into play as a table pedestal and art platform. Birdhouses and candles add fun decorative touches.

CARVE OUT A VIEW

A keyhole vista at Vancouver Island's Butchart Gardens shows how a simple bit of shrub removal can reveal a world beyond.

TAKE A PEEK. You can create your own garden window by cutting out a section of a hedge such as arborvitae or boxwood. Make sure there is a suitable focal point beyond your window. If not, create one of your own.

HIDEAWAY HOW-TO

Carve out a rustic retreat in your own backyard

A LASH IT. To create a natural picket fence, lash saplings to existing trees using rope or plastic ties. Lash the fence at the top and bottom to ensure its stability.

B GROUP IT. A semicircle of live and cut trees makes a rustic shell for this woodland retreat.

Less Is More
Disappearing Act

BEFORE

Creative Cover-Ups

TIME NEEDED
1 to 2 HOURS

Learn the landscaping sleight of hand that allows you to transform the unattractive into the amazing by just covering it up.

AFTER!
An unattractive (and difficult to mow around) well cap in this rural yard becomes a floral focal point by fitting a barn cupola over the top of the cap and surrounding it with a rock-lined bed overflowing with hydrangeas.

Some homeowners get to select the elements of their yard, but many inherit them when they buy a house. So many gardeners find themselves in the position of having to landscape around certain modern conveniences, such as central air-conditioning units, LP tanks, utility meters, and other protuberances of the landscape they may find visually unappealing. There are two basic ways to disguise the unattractive—you can hide it or you can enhance it.

ENHANCE IT

For years, these homeowners lived with a well cap in the center of the yard (left). The house and yard of this several-acre rural property previously depended on the water from a deep well. Once the property joined a rural water system, the well was capped, but a concrete pad was left in the center of the lawn—an unavoidable and unattractive focal point. The expense of filling in the well posed a problem, so the homeowners decided to hide the well cap and enhance the area around it with plantings. Because the homeowners liked the rustic style of their property, they looked for an accent that would support that look. They found an old barn cupola that was the perfect disguise for the well cap. They created a planting bed around the cupola, dressing up the base with large plantings of hydrangea shrubs that will grow several feet tall, providing a permanent and low-maintenance planting bed. Until the hydrangeas grow to maturity and fill in the area, the bed will be planted with colorful annuals.

HIDE IT

Any homeowner with central air-conditioning has to contend with the placement of a large humming box (below) somewhere in the landscape. This homeowner found that hiding it was the best solution. Several sections of unpainted lattice corralled the air-conditioning unit away from view. Then, in keeping with the garden design—which was whimsical—the homeowner added decorative stone finials on top of the screen to turn what was meant to be a disguise into an interesting addition to the overall landscape scheme.

DEALING WITH ON-GROUND DISTURBANCES—SAFETY FIRST

Many properties have a utilitarian object in the yard—an electrical box, a well cap, an LP tank, a water meter. Before you do any landscaping quick fixes, first make sure that it's safe to do so. Contact the appropriate utility company (power, gas, water) to learn of any restrictions it may have.

NOW YOU SEE IT, NOW YOU DON'T

There are many creative options for disguising the view of less-than-beautiful objects in your yard.

SCREEN IT. Using fence or lattice panels from a home improvement store, create a freestanding screen that hides the electrical box behind.

CALL ATTENTION TO IT. If the object is in a central spot of the yard, confront it head on and make it into a focal point. Add decorative post caps to add a flourish to your disguise.

PLANT AROUND IT. Hedge around it with boxwood or plant a screen of columnar arborvitae, or add a taller hedge. Plant a wide bed of hydrangea in front of it.

COVER IT UP. A chair, an overturned pot with another on top, a large, hollow-based finial or other decorative found object are all great ways to cover up a small inground object. You can even buy fake, hollow stones that are made for the specific purpose of covering up things like water meters.

Air-conditioning units are unlikely to fit any garden design. This smoke-and-mirrors diversion is created with lattice panels and stone finials.

PART
#3

PART
#1

PART
#2

Stream Water Garden in a Weekend

If nature neglected to grace your yard with a natural water feature, you can correct that oversight in a couple of days.

A water garden can be the unifying focal point of your yard. But a water feature is more than just a visual feast. It produces a natural multimedia experience: Sound, scent, color, reflection, and movement are all sensual qualities of a water garden.

Traditional inground ponds are perfect for homeowners with flat yards. The streambed water garden, however, gives hope to those with a slope. In fact, a slope is the perfect place to install a streambed water garden. With the same materials used in traditional pond-type water gardens, you can create a natural-looking streambed in your yard in only a few days.

STREAM DREAMS
One of the magical aspects of a natural stream is that moving water seems to take on a life of its own. It is water that is going somewhere, sparkling in the sun, eddying around stones, falling with purpose over the rise of large stones. In short, a stream is water that is alive.

You can create a streambed water garden that stops and starts wherever you want—thanks to the ingenuity of a recirculating pump. The pump keeps the stream's water moving from the still-water top, down the cascading rocks, to the bottom of the stream, where it is pumped back up via an underground tube.

LET THERE BE WATER
You can have a streambed water garden in a weekend. That includes digging out the area, unrolling the liner, setting the rocks, spreading gravel, installing the pump system, and planting the sides so that the streambed looks as though it has always been there.

THE GEOMETRY OF SLOPES
Any site with a slope of 1 inch per 10 feet will support a stream, but a greater slope expands the possibilities for building waterfalls. The waterfalls, each built with a different drop and producing a different sound, create music in the garden. Keeping the waterfalls in scale with the slope is important. Follow nature's lead. Departing from that scale will look (and sound) unnatural.

STREAM-PLANNING CHECKLIST
Before you add a water feature to your property, be sure to:

IDENTIFY UNDERGROUND UTILITIES AND EASEMENTS. Build the stream on your property rather than in the easements, and know where utilities are buried before you start planning.

CHECK ON BUILDING PERMITS. In most areas, building codes for swimming pools apply to water features.

THINK ABOUT WIRING NEEDS. Plan ahead to enjoy your stream after dark. Decide where you want nighttime lighting, and plan for its wiring along with that of your pump.

PLAN TRUCK ACCESS. A large dump truck will need a place to deliver several tons of gravel and stone.

Case Study
Streambed

GETTING THE LOOK

THE STREAM
- PVC return water pipe
- Recirculating pump
- Spun-polyester underlayment
- 45mm rubber liner

THE ROCKS
- Large stones
- Medium stones
- Small stones
- Gravel

THE PLANTS
- Water plants
- Edging plants

Part One:
The Process

TIME NEEDED
2 to 4 DAYS

You can have a stream garden up and running, looking and sounding just like the real thing.

1 DIG THE STREAM. The distance of the stream, called the stream run, and the end of the pond (the holding tank for water and the pump) are dug first. To make the stream fit into the landscape, have it wind around existing trees, shrubs, and plantings.

2 CREATE EVEN STREAM SIDES. In order for the water to flow downward without splashing over the sides, the two banks of the stream must be level with each other. The width and number of drop-offs (tiny waterfalls) can vary.

3 LINE THE BED. After the streambed is dug, line the bed with a spun polyester underlayment, then top with a 45mm rubber liner.

4 POSITION THE BIG ROCKS. The largest rocks are set into place to create the structure for the stream and to stabilize its edges.

5 ADD SMALLER STONES. Look at a real stream for inspiration, and you'll see stones of all sizes. Add small rocks and gravel to cover the entire surface of the streambed liner. Small stones look more natural, hide the liner, and offer surface areas for beneficial bacteria and algae that help keep the water clean.

6 ADD THE RETURN PIPE. The PVC return pipe carries the water from the bottom back up to the top—making the whole stream a recirculating action. The pipe is buried about 8 inches deep along the outside of the stream.

7 INSTALL THE PUMP. Use manufacturer's steps to install the pump.

EXPERT TIP
Take a design tip from nature when charting out your water garden stream. Rivers and creeks are never straight, so your stream should be laid out in something other than a straight line if it is going to look natural. Design a meandering, serpentine course that looks more like the real thing.

Case Study
Streambed

Boulders

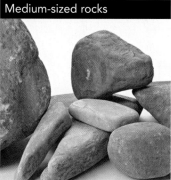
Medium-sized rocks

Small stones

Gravel

Part Two: The Rundown on Rocks

The key to creating a natural-looking stream is to combine rocks of all sizes—just as nature does—to create the streambed edges. You can have rock delivered for your project in the specifications and weights that you want.

WATERFALLS

One of the most relaxing aspects of a stream water garden is the sound of moving water. Small waterfalls installed along the streambed allow the water to create a music of its own. Here are some guidelines for creating waterfalls:

CONSULT NATURE. Take a look at natural waterfalls to see how the water flows around and over the rocks.

CREATE A WATER SYMPHONY. Vary the waterfall drop heights in your stream. The height that the water drops to the next level determines the sound that the water makes.

CREATE A SPLASH. Use a variety of materials to make unique waterfalls. Flat stones create curtains of water that flow to the next level. Rounded stones create bubbling sounds as the water flows over and around them. Hollowed tree trunks with water flowing through make a soft trickling sound.

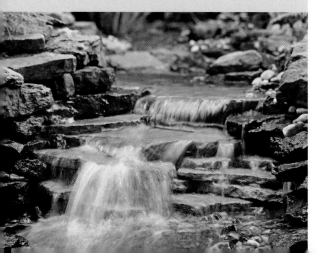

Mixing different types of stones, from boulders to gravel, makes any water feature look more natural. To create visual continuity between your water garden and surrounding areas, use the same type of stone in other landscaping projects, such as garden edging.

BOULDERS

Large rocks, some weighing several hundred pounds, are the framework of the stream bed. Irregularly shaped rocks can create a natural-looking outline. Look for different colors of stone (such as granite) to provide a variation of color. Boulder placement should be random—as if they were tossed there by a glacier. A string-of-pearls effect will look unrealistic, so use the boulders as the basis and support system for the streambed and let the smaller rocks fill in.

MEDIUM-SIZED ROCKS

Midrange rocks—roughly the size of bowling balls and smaller—serve as connecting puzzle pieces. Placement of medium-sized stones gives scale to the boulders and adds a sense of depth and reality to the streambed by breaking up the symmetry created when the boulders are placed in parallel rows to create the streambed.

SMALL STONES

Sprinkle small stones around the boulders and medium-sized rocks to offer scale. Small stones can be used as natural grout to full in holes and to cover any areas where the liner is poking through.

GRAVEL

Use smaller stones and gravel to fill the bottom of the streambed. This placement keeps the liner from showing, assumes the look of a real creek bed, and creates a natural stone mosaic over which the water flows.

Part Three: Streamside Plantings

Adding a mix of foliage and flowering plantings alongside a newly installed streambed water garden makes it look instantly established.

Daffodil

Bleeding heart

Hosta

Azalea

DAFFODILS (*NARCISSUS* SPP.)
Daffodils, tulips, frittilaria, and other small spring-blooming bulbs can be tucked around the streambed in the fall to create an instant woodland look the following spring when they are the first flowers to bloom in your yard.

BLEEDING HEART (*DICENTRA* SPP.)
Perennials such as bleeding heart offer long, arching stems that look fantastic leaning over a streambed water garden. This early spring-blooming perennial does best in shade and light shade and shows off delicate heart-shaped blooms that are suspended from arching stems like gems on a necklace.

HOSTA (*HOSTA* SPP.)
Hostas are the perfect shade-loving perennials for streambed water gardens. They have a mounding growth habit and range in size from petite to mammoth. Blue-hued varieties, such as 'Krossa Regal' or *hosta sieboldiana* 'Elegans' look especially nice planted near the water.

AZALEA (*RHODODENDRON VASEYI* SPP.)
One of the first shrubs to bloom in the spring, azaleas come in a stunning variety of bloom colors—from hot pink to delicate pink to white. Flowers measure about 1½ to 2¼ inches across. Bright-colored blossoms are reflected in the water and make elegant additions to both stream and in-ground water gardens.

ROOTED WATER PLANTINGS

Bog plants grow with their roots in the water. Many varieties are available, and they make perfect streamside plantings.

Horsetail

Water lily

Pickerel rush

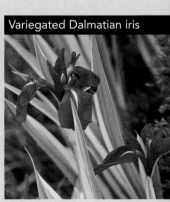
Variegated Dalmatian iris

HORSETAIL (*EQUISETUM* SPP.)
Available in standard and dwarf sizes, this grasslike reed has segmented hollow stems. *E. hyemale* grows 3 feet tall. The dwarf variety, *E. scirpoides*, grows just 6 inches tall. It prefers to grow in less than 2 inches of water or moist soil.

WATER LILY (*NYMPHAEA* SPP.)
Waterlily options include tropical and hardy, day-blooming and night-blooming, standard and miniature. Water lilies need still water, so when planted in a stream water garden, they should be placed in an area where their flat, surface-floating leaves will be protected from buffeting by waves or splashing.

PICKEREL WEED (*PONTEDERIA CORDATA*)
This attractive rush grows up to 30 inches tall and can be planted in water up to 12 inches deep. It blooms in late spring and early fall, producing spires of bright blue flowers.

WATER IRISES—YELLOW FLAG IRIS (*IRIS PSEUDACORUS*), JAPANESE IRIS (*IRIS ENSATA*), AND OTHERS
Tucked into the bank or in shallow water, water irises produce large stands of spiky-leaved foliage topped with yellow, blue, or white flowers. Plants grow up to 48 inches tall and can be planted in moist soil at the water's edge or in water up to 10 inches deep. They bloom in early to late spring, depending on variety.

Case Study
Lush Shade Garden

PART
#1

PART
#2

Turn an overgrown wooded lot into a woodland oasis. Perennials, annuals, trees, and shrubs form a backdrop of living color for a path that winds leisurely among bloom-filled beds.

Deep shade in the garden stymies many homeowners—grass refuses to grow and sun-loving flowers struggle toward light. But the phrase "made in the shade" has never been more apt than in shade gardening—wonderful species of plants would grow less well anywhere else. Hostas love deep shade. Solomon's seal happily arches the way it does with most success in leafy darkness. And shy woodland wildflowers will shrivel in more lighted areas. When you look to the dark side, you'll find a wide array of interesting options for planting. And with the right design and plants, you can transform a shady problem space into a flower-filled wonderland.

Part One:
Creating a Path

Where some people might see a nettle-infested lot, this homeowner envisioned a meandering path running past overflowing beds of colorful flowers.

1 CLEAR THE SPACE. Clear the brush, keeping plants with wildlife appeal such as honeysuckle vines, junipers, blackberries, silver and Norway maples, serviceberries, wild anise, and Jacob's ladder.

2 TILL THE PATH. Rototill a 5-inch-deep meandering path and line it with landscape fabric. Cover the mat with 4 inches of chopped brick, which is easy to maintain and walk on. To accommodate planting beds on both sides of the path, enrich the existing soil with a top dressing of loam.

3 CREATE A DRY STREAMBED LOOK. Line the planting areas with rocks of varying sizes.

4 ADD FOOTLIGHT PLANTINGS. To lighten the area along the pathway, use light-colored annuals that will take hold and bloom all summer. Plant perennials such as goatsbeard and anemone for white flowers.

LOOSE STONE PAVING OPTIONS

For an informal pathway through the woods, the best medium is loose stone. It drains easily, is low cost, and creates a fairly non-slip surface—something to consider when covering a sloping area. In addition, these materials come in a range of sizes and colors, so you can create the look you want. Best of all, they are easy to install—just shovel them into place.

• Layer gravel about 2 inches deep for adequate coverage.

• Gravel that is about ¾ inches in diameter is the easiest to walk on.

• Install edging to prevent people and dogs from scattering small stones such as pea gravel into the garden.

• Hosing down gravel makes it look fresh and clean. In the early spring, a brief raking will unearth leaves and small branches for easy removal.

• For small paths, buy gravel in bags; for larger jobs, buy it by the ton.

• Crushed oyster shells are a traditional medium for paths. Broken shells provide a firm walking surface.

SHOPPING LIST

GETTING THE LOOK

THE PATH
- Landscape cloth
- Chipped brick
- Edging stones

THE BEDS
- 2 flats pink impatiens
- 2 flats white impatiens
- 2 pagoda dogwoods
- Redbud
- 3 yews
- 3 arrowwood viburnums
- 6 hostas

Lily-of-the-valley

Goatsbeard

Fern

Jack-in-the-pulpit

Ajuga

Scilla

Vinca

Bleeding heart

Part Two: Plants Made for the Shade

You can brighten a dark spot in your yard with any of a variety of shade-loving species.

GROUND-COVERS

For a patch of lawn that's mostly bare soil under a tree, try filling in the gaps with a groundcover. These shallow-rooted plants can survive in the sparse soil on top of tree roots.

LILY-OF-THE-VALLEY
(CONVALLARIA MAJALIS)

ENGLISH IVY
(HEDERA HELIX)

STAR JASMINE
(TRACHELOSPER-MUM ASIATICUM)

PERIWINKLE
(VINCA MAJOR)

BLUE LILYTURF
(LIRIOPE MUSCARI)

SPOTTED DEADNETTLE
(LAMIUM MACULATUM)

WINTER CREEPER
(EUONYMUS FORTUNEI)

AJUGA
(AJUGA REPTANS)

SHRUBS

Shrubs add structure to a garden path and create great habitats for birds. Many flower in spring and produce berries in autumn that are as appealing to humans as to the bird species that come to dine.

JAPANESE PIERIS
(PIERIS JAPONICA)

JAPANESE AUCUBA
(AUCUBA JAPONICA)

CAMELLIA
(CAMELLIA SPP.)

CORALBERRY
(SYMPHORICARPOS ORBICULATUS)

HOLLY
(ILEX SPP.)

OREGON GRAPEHOLLY
(MAHONIA AQUIFOLIUM)

AZALEA
(RHODODENDRON SPP.)

ANNUALS

Light up the pathways with bright-blooming flower-and-foliage annuals. These beauties will stay in bloom all summer long, providing color and light in shady beds.

NEW GUINEA IMPATIENS
(IMPATIENS HAWKERI)

BEGONIA
(BEGONIA SPP.)

COLEUS
(SOLENOSTEMON SCUTELLARIOIDES)

IMPATIENS
(IMPATIENS SPP.)

BULBS

For every season there are bulbs that relish a safe and shady spot. Plan ahead for all-season color with these amazing options.

CALADIUM
(CALADIUM BICOLOR) (summer blooming)

NARCISSUS
(NARCISSUS SPP.)
(spring blooming)

AUTUMN CROCUS
(COLCHICUM SPP.)
(fall blooming)

PERENNIALS

To add height and texture to shady areas, look to the amazing possibilities of flower and foliage from shade-loving perennials. Clustered together—as they might grow in nature—ferns add lacy texture, hostas offer leafy lushness, and columbines add dots of waving color.

COLUMBINE
(AQUILEGIA SPP.)

PHLOX (PHLOX SPP.)

VIOLETS (VIOLA SPP.)

BLEEDING HEART
(DICENTRA SPP.)

GOATSBEARD
(ARUNCUS DIOICUS)

JACK-IN-THE-PULPIT
(ARISAEMA TRIPHYLLUM)

HOSTA (HOSTA SPP.)

FERN (holly fern, painted fern, royal fern, sensitive fern, wood fern, autumn fern, river fern)

Case Study
Front Yard Facelift

Part
#3

Part
#2

Part
#1

Fresh landscaping breathes new life into a plain front yard—improving the
curb appeal and real estate value. The view from the street sets the style
for the rest of the house.

urb appeal. It's the crucial opportunity for
your home to make a good first impression.
Whether you are sprucing up your yard to
make your home an easy seller on the market
or giving it a much-needed overhaul that you plan to
enjoy yourself, enhancing the landscaping at the front of
your home always provides an added lift—both
financially and inspirationally.

1

2

LANDSCAPING INCREASES REAL ESTATE VALUE

According to several polls and studies, landscaping increases the value of your home. The Gallup Organization indicates that landscaping can add up to 15 percent to a home's value. For a house selling for $200,000, that's $30,000. The Council of Tree & Landscape Appraisers indicates that a mature tree can often have an appraised value of between $1,000 and $10,000. Of course, the big benefit for homeowners with a nicely landscaped yard is the "coming home" feeling of a beautifully planted yard.

RESCUING THE RAMBLING RANCH

This front-yard facelift was completed in three steps: a new walkway, a front step makeover, and planting bed additions. The austere facade of this ranch house needed a refigured walkway as well as a floral facelift. New curving pathways softened the harsh lines of the rectangular house. A simple glued-on brick coat for unattractive and outmoded concrete steps added instant impact even before the glue dried. And generous planting beds added a growing space for a colorful assortment of trees, shrubs, and flowers.

3

Part One:
Build a Stone Wall

TIME NEEDED
2 to 4 DAYS

Because the front yard slopes slightly away from the front door, it's important to make planting beds level on both sides of the path.

1 BEFORE. This ranch-style home had outdated landscaping that consisted of a couple of contractor-installed junipers.

2 BUILD THE BED. The easiest way to level a sloping planting bed is to add soil. Add the soil dug out from the pathway. Then dig a low, level trench along the perimeter of each garden bed.

3 LAY THE WALL STONE. Position the 4-inch-thick limestone end to end in the trench. After the first layer of stone is set, add more stone, alternating each row so the spaces between the stones are staggered.

4 BACKFILL THE AREA WITH SOIL. Till in several bales of sphagnum peat moss to make the bed easier to plant in. If necessary, amend the soil with other organic materials.

4

 SHOPPING LIST

GETTING THE LOOK

THE WALL
- Wall stone
- Soil
- Impatiens
- *Sedum* 'Autumn Joy'

THE PATH
- Aggregate
- Sand
- Brick
- Brick edging

THE STEPS
- Bricks
- All-weather epoxy

Part Two:
Install the Path

Laying a professional-looking path may be easier than you think. Here are the steps, which also work for laying a patio.

1 MARK YOUR SPOT. Mark the location of the path with white spray paint. Remove the sod by hand or with a sod stripper. Use a spade to excavate to a depth of 7 inches.

2 SPREAD A BASE. Spread a 4-inch base of aggregate over the surface of the path. Rent a plate compactor to level the material. This provides a solid and even surface for the brick.

3 ADD SAND. After the aggregate is in place, cover it with an inch of coarse sand. Rake the sand level but avoid packing it down because bricks are easier to lay in loose sand.

4 CLEAR BEDS. Remove sod to create the area for the planting beds. Amend the soil with peat moss.

5 INSERT BRICK EDGING. Edge the path with a commercial brick edging that creates a rigid edge to keep your bricks in position—especially on a curve.

6 POSITION BRICKS. Place the bricks on the sand starting along the path's edge. Then, position the rest of the bricks. Add a layer of sand over the bricks and tamp down with a plate compactor.

HOW TO HIRE PROFESSIONALS
When you need to bring in professional help, ask the right questions to make sure you are getting reliable and experienced people to do the job.

PROFESSIONAL LANDSCAPER CHECKLIST
- How long has the landscaper been in business?
- Will he provide a written quote with materials/labor specified?
- When will work begin?
- How long will the job take?
- Can the landscaper finish by a certain date?
- Will the landscaper provide references?

AFTER!

Part Three: Camouflage Concrete

Concrete steps often crack after a few years. A quick glue-and-brick upgrade steps up the style.

For many older homes with concrete steps, there comes a time when the surface of the concrete, and perhaps the edges, starts looking a little the worse for wear. The steps themselves are still structurally sound, so refacing rather than replacement is possible. A brick facade was the perfect solution for updating the look of these steps without the cost of replacement.

BEFORE

1 REPAIR any surface cracks or uneven edges on the porch and steps before applying the brick facade.

2 BUY THE APPROPRIATE NUMBER OF BRICKS to recover the steps and platform. Because bricks are being glued into position rather than mortared, it's important to select bricks that have completely even surfaces.

3 POSITION THE BRICKS onto the porch in the pattern that looks best based on the size and shape of the steps. Align the bricks flush with the edge of the steps; allowing the brick to overhang the edge of the step could results in stepping pressure loosening it over time.

4 LIFT UP EACH BRICK, apply a generous amount of all-weather epoxy to the step, and position it in place. Continue until the entire surface of the porch, including the steps, has been covered.

Sedum 'Autumn Joy'

Impatiens

Potted mum

Hosta

PICKING THE RIGHT PLANTS

Mixing annuals and perennials in a new landscape brings you instant impact color and long-term blooms.

SEDUM 'AUTUMN JOY'

This hardy perennial produces thick chartreuse leaves. In early autumn, umbels of russet blooms color the landscape. 'Autumn Joy' is a tall-growing perennial, attaining heights of about 2 feet. Leave the flower heads on the plant for all-winter interest.

IMPATIENS

Available in white, pink, fuchsia, orange, and some bicolors, impatiens are annuals that love shady spots. For a newly landscaped bed, buy impatiens by the flat and space them just inches apart. In hot weather, they wilt easily, so keep them well watered.

POTTED MUM

Add color anywhere you need it in your landscape by potting up containers of bright-blooming mums. Available in a wide range of colors and sizes, these hardy fall-flowering perennials will take a light frost and keep on blooming.

HOSTA

Shade-loving perennials, hostas fill in a landscape bed with their large leaves and lush foliage. In the late summer, they produce long spires topped with delicate, trumpet-shaped blooms. Hostas come in varieties from 4 inches to 2 feet tall.

LANDSCAPING KNOW-HOW

Making the right plant choices for your landscape pays off in the long run. Planting them in a space where they will flourish is also important.

1 CHOOSE THE RIGHT PLANT FOR THE RIGHT PLACE. When shopping for plants, refer to their labels for important care information. Plant tags will tell you what zones the plant will grow in, the mature size of the species, its light requirements, and how much you should water it. Care tips and fertilization requirements may also be listed.

2 SPACE ACCORDING TO SIZE. Although shrubs may appear small, they will grow, so space them to accommodate their mature width and height. Here, dwarf yews are planted 3 feet away from the house's foundation. When you place shrubs or groundcovers near foundations, avoid planting under eaves and gutters. If you are aiming for a lusher look by planting shrubs closer together than recommended, plan to do some extra pruning.

3 MEASURE FOR CORRECT PLANTING WIDTHS. Each shrub or tree has a mature width, which is what the planting tag's spacing recommendations are based upon. The junipers here are planted 3 feet apart. Larger, spreading deciduous shrubs should be spaced 4 to 5 feet apart.

4 DIG BIG. When planting a tree or shrub, dig the planting hole larger than the root ball of the plant. Then remove the plant from its pot (or remove the burlap and wire covering on balled-and-burlapped plants) and lower it into the hole. Be sure to set the shrub or tree at the same level it was growing previously. To keep newly planted shrubs in good health, mulch around their bases and keep them well watered.

For more information on where to find lawn and gardening supplies, outdoor furniture, garden lighting equipment, problem solving, water garden equipment and supplies, and water garden design and installation services featured in this book, consult the following websites:

BECKETT CORPORATION
This manufacturer of water garden equipment and supplies maintains an informative website full of project ideas, design tips, installation techniques, and frequently asked questions.
WWW.888BECKETT.COM

AQUASCAPE DESIGNS
Use this website to locate a contractor near you for water garden design and installation services. Here you will also find a lively image gallery of design ideas as well as useful tips for installation and maintenance.
WWW.AQUASCAPEDESIGNS.COM

SCOTTS
North America's premier manufacturer of lawn care supplies maintains a lively and informative website on the basics of growing the perfect lawn, including numerous how-to videos and a free email newsletter.
WWW.SCOTTS.COM

ORTHO
Ortho's bug finder and weed finder helps you identify and solve nearly every garden problem there is with the Ortho Problem Solver on-line. Includes free e-mail gardening tips.
WWW.ORTHO.COM

SMITH & HAWKEN
Whether you're looking for the best tools, outdoor furniture, garden art, containers, garden supplies, plants, or clothing to garden in, this website is loaded with products and ideas.
WWW.SMITHANDHAWKEN.COM

INTERMATIC
This manufacturer of home garden lighting equipment under the well-known Malibu brand also produces outdoor lighting equipment marketed to professionals. This website contains a wealth of product information as well as installation instructions, design tips, and equipment manuals on garden lighting.
WWW.INTERMATIC.COM

 www.miraclegro.com

For more information on how to grow successfully, go to www.miracle-gro.com where you'll find:

- **Miracle-Gro Garden Helpline:** 800/645-8166

- **More Exciting Project Ideas**

- **Special Gardening Tips From Peter Strauss**

- **Step-by Step Instructions for Basic Gardening Techniques**

- **Email Reminder Service:** Free gardening tips and reminders sent to you via email.

- **Miracle-Gro Product Consumer Guide:** The latest information on all Miracle-Gro products, including plant foods, soil mixes, and exciting new product lines from Miracle-Gro.

- **Garden Problem Solver:** Link into a comprehensive library of diagnostic tools and solutions for insect, disease, and weed problems.

- **Streaming How-to Videos:** Click into a library of more than 50 quick gardening and lawn-care video clips.

USDA Plant Hardiness Zone Map

This map of climate zones helps you select plants for your garden that will survive a typical winter in your region. The United States Department of Agriculture (USDA) developed the map, basing the zones on the lowest recorded temperatures across North America. Zone 1 is the coldest area and Zone 11 is the warmest.

Plants are classified by the coldest temperature and zone they can endure. For example, plants hardy to Zone 6 survive where winter temperatures drop to –10° F. Those hardy to Zone 8 die long before it's that cold. These plants may grow in colder regions but must be replaced each year. Plants rated for a range of hardiness zones can usually survive winter in the coldest region as well as tolerate the summer heat of the warmest one.

To find your hardiness zone, note the approximate location of your community on the map, then match the color band marking that area to the key.

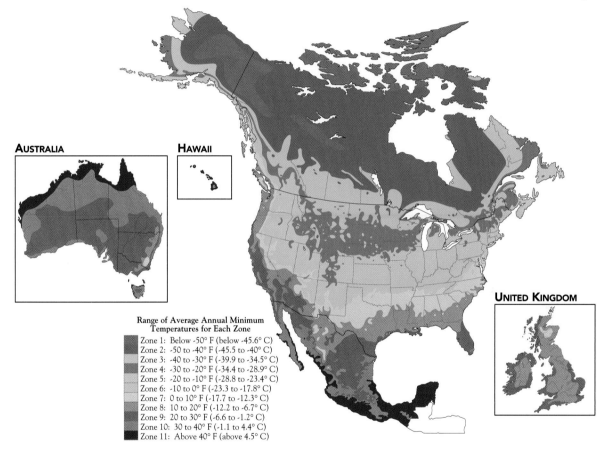

AUSTRALIA

HAWAII

UNITED KINGDOM

Range of Average Annual Minimum Temperatures for Each Zone

Zone 1: Below -50° F (below -45.6° C)
Zone 2: -50 to -40° F (-45.5 to -40° C)
Zone 3: -40 to -30° F (-39.9 to -34.5° C)
Zone 4: -30 to -20° F (-34.4 to -28.9° C)
Zone 5: -20 to -10° F (-28.8 to -23.4° C)
Zone 6: -10 to 0° F (-23.3 to -17.8° C)
Zone 7: 0 to 10° F (-17.7 to -12.3° C)
Zone 8: 10 to 20° F (-12.2 to -6.7° C)
Zone 9: 20 to 30° F (-6.6 to -1.2° C)
Zone 10: 30 to 40° F (-1.1 to 4.4° C)
Zone 11: Above 40° F (above 4.5° C)

METRIC CONVERSIONS

U.S. Units to Metric Equivalents			Metric Units to U.S. Equivalents		
To Convert From	**Multiply By**	**To Get**	**To Convert From**	**Multiply By**	**To Get**
Inches	25.4	Millimeters	Millimeters	0.0394	Inches
Inches	2.54	Centimeters	Centimeters	0.3937	Inches
Feet	30.48	Centimeters	Centimeters	0.0328	Feet
Feet	0.3048	Meters	Meters	3.2808	Feet
Yards	0.9144	Meters	Meters	1.0936	Yards

To convert from degrees Fahrenheit (F) to degrees Celsius (C), first subtract 32, then multiply by ⅝.

To convert from degrees Celsius to degrees Fahrenheit, multiply by ⅝, then add 32.

Instant Gardens
Project Editor: Michael McKinley
Contributing Designers: Brad and Sundie Ruppert
Contributing Writer: Karen Weir Jimerson
Contributing Technical Editors for Miracle-Gro: David Slaybaugh,
    Lisa Zierten, Rich Foster, Jennifer Anderson
Photographers: Marty Baldwin, Scott Little, Blaine Moats, Jay Wilde
Contributing Prop/Photo Stylists: Studio G
Copy Chief: Terri Fredrickson
Contributing Copy Editors: Linda Armstrong
Technical Proofreader: Fran Gardner
Contributing Proofreaders: Julie Cahalan, Elsa Kramer
Publishing Operations Manager: Karen Schirm
Senior Editor, Asset and Information Manager: Phillip Morgan
Edit and Design Production Coordinator: Mary Lee Gavin
Editorial and Design Assistant: Kathleen Stevens
Book Production Managers: Pam Kvitne, Marjorie J. Schenkelberg,
    Rick von Holdt, Mark Weaver
Contributing Map Illustrator: Jana Fothergill

Meredith® Books
Executive Director, Editorial: Gregory H. Kayko
Executive Director, Design: Matt Strelecki
Managing Editor: Amy Tincher-Durik
Executive Editor/Group Manager: Benjamin W. Allen
Senior Associate Design Director: Tom Wegner
Marketing Product Manager: Brent Wiersma

Publisher and Editor in Chief: James D. Blume
Editorial Director: Linda Raglan Cunningham
Executive Director, New Business Development:
    Todd M. Davis
Executive Director, Sales: Ken Zagor
Director, Operations: George A. Susral
Director, Production: Douglas M. Johnston
Director, Marketing: Amy Nichols
Business Director: Jim Leonard

Vice President and General Manager: Douglas J. Guendel

Meredith Publishing Group
President: Jack Griffin
Executive Vice President: Bob Mate

Meredith Corporation
Chairman and Chief Executive Officer: William T. Kerr
President and Chief Operating Officer: Stephen M. Lacy

In Memoriam: E.T. Meredith III (1933–2003)

All of us at Meredith® Books are dedicated to providing
you with the information and ideas you need to enhance your home
and garden. We welcome your comments and suggestions about this
book. Write to us at:
    Meredith Corporation
    Meredith Gardening Books
    1716 Locust St.
    Des Moines, IA 50309–3023

Thanks to: Janet Anderson, Beckett Water Gardens,
Nate Carder, Susan Ferguson, The Fireplace Superstore,
Donna Fjelland, Harvey's Greenhouse and Floral,
Heard Gardens, Lou Lyle Craftsman, Judy Milligan-McCarty,
Vern Reynolds, Rhino Materials, Shirley Ruppert,
Stark Gardens, Brenda Witherspoon,

Additional Photography:
    (Photographers credited may retain copyright © to the
    listed photographs)
L = Left, R = Right, C = Center, B = Bottom, T = Top
Liz Ball/Positive Images: 117B; Phillipe Bonduel/Garden
    PictureLibrary: 121BRC;
Ken Druse: 144T, 145L, 155L;
Derek Fell: 123L, 154, 155R, 160TL, 165T;
GardenWorld Images: 117TC;
Jerry Harpur: 22T, 22B, 152TL, 152BL, 160BL,
Jerry Harpur, Design: Steve Martino: 21T, 21B, 152BR, 158B,
Jerry Harpur, Design Johnstone Bourne Partnership: 23,
Jerry Harpur, Design Jimmie Morrison: 144B,
Jerry Harpur, Design John & Kathleen Holmes: 158T,
Jerry Harpur, Design Michael Von Valkenburgh: 160TR,
Jerry Harpur, Design Piet Oudolf: 160BR;
Marcus Harpur, Design Jim Honey & James Dyson: 20,
    152TR
Marcus Harpur, Design Justin Greer: 135L,
Marcus Harpur, Design Piet Oudolf: 145R;
Dency Kane: 173BR;
Rosemary Kautzky: 117TR;
Andrew Lawson: 114T, 115T, 115BLC;
Chuck Mitchell: 119;
Howard Rice/Garden Picture Library: 117TRC
Susan Roth: 109TR;
Neil Soderstrom: 117TLC;
Pam Spaulding/Positive Images: 110B;
Michael Thompson: 115BL, 127L, 173BL;
Justyn Willsmore: 117TL